The Pocket EMMA GOLDMAN

The Pocket
EMMA GOLDMAN

Trident Press
Boulder, CO

All of Goldman's essays included in this collection are edited versions of those in the Anarchist Library.

Published by Trident Press
940 Pearl St.
Boulder, CO 80302

tridentcafe.com

ISBN: 978-0-9992499-7-0

Contents

The Failure of Christianity

The counterfeiters and poisoners of ideas, in their attempt to obscure the line between truth and falsehood, find a valuable ally in the conservatism of language.

Conceptions and words that have long ago lost their original meaning continue through centuries to dominate mankind. Especially is this true if these conceptions have become a common-place, if they have been instilled in our beings from our infancy as great and irrefutable verities. The average mind is easily content with inherited and acquired things, or with the dicta of parents and teachers, because it is much easier to imitate than to create.

Our age has given birth to two intellectual giants, who have undertaken to transvalue the dead social and moral values of the past, especially those contained in Christianity. Friedrich Nietzsche and Max Stirner have hurled blow upon blow against the portals of Christianity, because they saw in it a pernicious slave morality, the denial of life, the destroyer of all the elements that make for strength and character. True, Nietzsche has opposed the slave-morality idea inherent in Christianity in behalf of a master morality for the privileged few. But I venture to suggest that his master idea had nothing to do with the vulgarity of station, caste, or wealth. Rather did it mean the masterful in human possibilities, the masterful in man that would help him to overcome old traditions and worn-out values, so that he may learn to become the creator of new and beautiful things.

Both Nietzsche and Stirner saw in Christianity the leveler of the human race, the breaker of man's will to dare and to do. They saw in every movement built on Christian morality and ethics attempts not at the emancipation from slavery, but for the perpetuation thereof. Hence they opposed these movements with might and main.

Whether I do or do not entirely agree with these iconoclasts, I believe, with them, that Christianity is most admirably adapted to the training of slaves, to the perpetuation of a slave society; in short, to the very conditions confronting us today. Indeed, never could society have degenerated to its present appalling stage, if not for the assistance of Christianity. The rulers of the earth have realized long ago what potent poison inheres in the Christian religion. That is the reason they foster it; that is why they leave nothing undone to instill it into the blood of the people. They know only too well that the subtleness of the Christian teachings is a more powerful protection against rebellion and discontent than the club or the gun.

No doubt I will be told that, though religion is a poison and institutionalized Christianity the greatest enemy of progress and freedom, there is some good in Christianity "itself." What about the teachings of Christ and — early Christianity, I may be asked; do they not stand for the spirit of humanity, for right and justice?

It is precisely this oft-repeated contention that induced me to choose this subject, to enable me to demonstrate that the abuses of Christianity, like the abuses of government, are conditioned in the thing itself, and are not to be charged to the representatives of the creed. Christ and his teachings are the embodiment of submission, of inertia, of the denial of life; hence responsible for the things done in their name.

I am not interested in the theological Christ. Brilliant minds like Bauer, Strauss, Renan, Thomas Paine, and others refuted that myth long ago. I am even ready to admit that the theological Christ is not half so dangerous as the ethical and social Christ. In proportion as science takes the place of blind faith, theology loses its hold. But the ethical and poetical Christ-myth has so thoroughly saturated our lives that even some of the most advanced minds find it difficult to emancipate themselves from its yoke. They have rid themselves of the letter, but have retained the spirit; yet it is the spirit which is back of all the crimes and horrors committed by orthodox Christianity. The Fathers of the Church can well afford to preach the gospel of Christ. It contains nothing dangerous to the regime of authority and wealth; it stands for self-denial and self-abnegation, for penance and regret, and is absolutely inert in the face of every [in]dignity, every outrage imposed upon mankind.

Here I must revert to the counterfeiters of ideas and words. So many otherwise earnest haters of slavery and injustice confuse, in a most distressing manner, the teachings of Christ with the great struggles for social and economic emancipation. The two are irrevocably and forever opposed to each other. The one necessitates courage, daring, defiance, and strength. The other preaches the gospel of non-resistance, of slavish acquiescence in the will of others; it is the complete disregard of character and self-reliance, and therefore destructive of liberty and well-being.

Whoever sincerely aims at a radical change in society, whoever strives to free humanity from the scourge of dependence and misery, must turn his back on Christianity, on the old as well as the present form of the same.

Everywhere and always, since its very inception, Christianity has turned the earth into a vale of tears; always it has made of life a weak, diseased thing, always it has instilled fear in man, turning him into a dual being, whose life energies are spent in the struggle between body and soul. In decrying the body as something evil, the flesh as the tempter to everything that is sinful, man has mutilated his being in the vain attempt to keep his soul pure, while his body rotted away from the injuries and tortures inflicted upon it.

The Christian religion and morality extols the glory of the Hereafter, and therefore remains indifferent to the horrors of the earth. Indeed, the idea of self-denial and of all that makes for pain and sorrow is its test of human worth, its passport to the entry into heaven.

The poor are to own heaven, and the rich will go to hell. That may account for the desperate efforts of the rich to make hay while the sun shines, to get as much out of the earth as they can: to wallow in wealth and superfluity, to tighten their iron hold on the blessed slaves, to rob them of their birthright, to degrade and outrage them every minute of the day. Who can blame the rich if they revenge themselves on the poor, for now is their time, and the merciful Christian God alone knows how ably and completely the rich are doing it.

And the poor? They cling to the promise of the Christian heaven, as the home for old age, the sanitarium for crippled bodies and weak minds. They endure and submit, they suffer and wait, until every bit of self-respect has been knocked out of them, until their bodies become emaciated and withered, and their spirit broken from the wait, the weary endless wait for the Christian heaven.

Christ made his appearance as the leader of the people, the redeemer of the Jews from Roman dominion; but the moment he began his work, he proved that he had no interest in the earth, in the pressing immediate needs of the poor and the disinherited of his time. what he preached was a sentimental mysticism, obscure and confused ideas lacking originality and vigor.

When the Jews, according to the gospels, withdrew from Jesus, when they turned him over to the cross, they may have been bitterly disappointed in him who promised them so much and gave them so little. He promised joy and bliss in another world, while the people were starving, suffering, and enduring before his very eyes.

It may also be that the sympathy of the Romans, especially of Pilate, was given

Christ because they regarded him as perfectly harmless to their power and sway. The philosopher Pilate may have considered Christ's "eternal truths" as pretty anaemic and lifeless, compared with the array of strength and force they attempted to combat. The Romans, strong and unflinching as they were, must have laughed in their sleeves over the man who talked repentance and patience, instead of calling to arms against the despoilers and oppressors of his people.

The public career of Christ begins with the edict, "Repent, for the Kingdom of Heaven is at hand."

Why repent, why regret, in the face of something that was supposed to bring deliverance? Had not the people suffered and endured enough; had they not earned their right to deliverance by their suffering? Take the Sermon on the Mount, for instance. What is it but a eulogy on submission to fate, to the inevitability of things?

"Blessed are the poor in spirit, for

theirs is the Kingdom of Heaven."

Heaven must be an awfully dull place if the poor in spirit live there. How can anything creative, anything vital, useful and beautiful come from the poor in spirit? The idea conveyed in the Sermon on the Mount is the greatest indictment against the teachings of Christ, because it sees in the poverty of mind and body a virtue, and because it seeks to maintain this virtue by reward and punishment. Every intelligent being realizes that our worst curse is the poverty of the spirit; that it is productive of all evil and misery, of all the injustice and crimes in the world. Every one knows that nothing good ever came or can come of the poor in spirit; surely never liberty, justice, or equality.

"Blessed are the meek, for they shall inherit the earth."

What a preposterous notion! What incentive to slavery, inactivity, and parasitism! Besides, it is not true that the meek can inherit anything. Just because humanity has been meek, the earth has been stolen from it.

Meekness has been the whip, which capitalism and governments have used to force man into dependency, into his slave position. The most faithful servants of the State, of wealth, of special privilege, could not preach a more convenient gospel than did Christ, the "redeemer" of the people.

"Blessed are they that hunger and thirst for righteousness, for they shall be filled."

But did not Christ exclude the possibility of righteousness when he said, "The poor ye have always with you"? But, then, Christ was great on dicta, no matter if they were utterly opposed to each other. This is nowhere demonstrated so strikingly as in his command, "Render to Caesar the things that are Caesar's, and to God the things that are God's."

The interpreters claim that Christ had to make these concessions to the powers of his time. If that be true, this single compromise was sufficient to prove, down to this very day, a most ruthless weapon in the hands of the oppressor, a fearful lash and relentless tax-gatherer, to the impoverishment, the enslavement, and degradation of the very people for whom Christ is supposed to have died. And when we are assured that "Blessed are they that hunger and thirst for righteousness, for they shall be filled," are we told the how? How? Christ never takes the trouble to explain that. Righteousness does not come from the stars, nor because Christ willed it so. Righteousness grows out of liberty, of social and economic opportunity and equality. But how can the meek, the poor in spirit, ever establish such a state of affairs?

"Blessed are ye when men shall revile you and persecute you, and say all manner of evil against you falsely, for my sake. Rejoice, and be exceeding glad: for great is your reward in heaven."

The reward in heaven is the perpetual bait, a bait that has caught man in an iron net, a strait-jacket which does not let him expand or grow. All pioneers of truth have been, and still are, reviled; they have been, and still are, persecuted. But did they ask humanity to pay the price? Did they seek to bribe mankind to accept their ideas? They knew too well that he who accepts a truth because of the bribe, will soon barter it away to a higher bidder.

Good and bad, punishment and reward, sin and penance, heaven and hell, as the moving spirit of the Christ-gospel have been the stumbling-block in the world's work. It contains everything in the way of orders and commands, but entirely lacks the very things we need most.

The worker who knows the cause of his misery, who understands the make-up of our iniquitous social and industrial system can do more for himself and his kind than Christ and the followers of Christ have ever done for humanity; certainly more than meek patience, ignorance, and submission have done.

How much more ennobling, how much more beneficial is the extreme individualism of Stirner and Nietzsche than the sick-room atmosphere of the Christian faith. If they repudiate altruism as an evil, it is because of the example contained in Christianity, which set a premium on parasitism and inertia, gave birth to all manner of social disorders that are to be cured with the preachment of love and sympathy.

Proud and self-reliant characters prefer hatred to such sickening artificial love. Not because of any reward does a free spirit take his stand for a great truth, nor has such a one ever been deterred because of fear of punishment.

"Think not that I come to destroy the law or the prophets. I am not come to destroy, but to fulfill."

Precisely. Christ was a reformer, ever ready to patch up, to fulfill, to carry on the old order of things; never to destroy and rebuild. That may account for the fellow-feeling all reformers have for him.

Indeed, the whole history of the State, Capitalism, and the Church proves that they have perpetuated themselves because of the idea "I come not to destroy the law." This is the key to authority and oppression. Naturally so, for did not Christ praise poverty as a virtue; did he not propagate non-resistance to evil? Why should not poverty and evil continue to rule the world?

Much as I am opposed to every religion, much as I think them an imposition upon, and crime against, reason and progress, I yet feel that no other religion has done so much harm or has helped so much in the enslavement of man as the religion of Christ.

Witness Christ before his accusers. What lack of dignity, what lack of faith in himself and in his own ideas! So weak and helpless was this "Saviour of Men" that he must needs the whole human family to pay for him, unto all eternity, because he "hath died for them." Redemption through the Cross is worse than damnation, because of the terrible burden it imposes upon humanity, because of the effect it has on the human soul, fettering and paralyzing it with the weight of the burden exacted through the death of Christ.

Thousands of martyrs have perished, yet few, if any, of them have proved so helpless as the great Christian God. Thousands have gone to their death with greater fortitude, with more courage, with deeper faith in their ideas than the Nazarene. Nor did they expect eternal gratitude from their fellow-men because of what they endured for them.

Compared with Socrates and Bruno, with the great martyrs of Russia, with the Chicago Anarchists, Francisco Ferrer, and unnumbered others, Christ cuts a poor figure indeed. Compared with the delicate, frail Spiridonova who underwent the most terrible tortures, the most horrible indignities, without losing faith in herself or her cause, Jesus is a veritable nonentity. They stood their ground and faced their executioners with unffinching determination, and though they, too, died for the people, they asked nothing in return for their great sacrifice.

Verily, we need redemption from the

slavery, the deadening weakness, and humiliating dependency of Christian morality.

The teachings of Christ and of his followers have failed because they lacked the vitality to lift the burdens from the shoulders of the race; they have failed because the very essence of that doctrine is contrary to the spirit of life, exposed to the manifestations of nature, to the strength and beauty of passion.

Never can Christianity, under whatever mask it may appear — be it New Liberalism, Spiritualism, Christian Science, New Thought, or a thousand and one other forms of hysteria and neurasthenia — bring us relief from the terrible pressure of conditions, the weight of poverty, the horrors of our iniquitous system. Christianity is the conspiracy of ignorance against reason, of darkness against light, of submission and slavery against independence and freedom; of the denial of strength and beauty, against the affirmation of the joy and glory of life.

The Philosophy of Atheism

To give an adequate exposition of the Philosophy of Atheism, it would be necessary to go into the historical changes of the belief in a Deity, from its earliest beginning to the present day. But that is not within the scope of the present paper. However, it is not out of place to mention, in passing, that the concept God, Supernatural Power, Spirit, Deity, or in whatever other term the essence of Theism may have found expression, has become more indefinite and obscure in the course of time and progress. In other words, the God idea is growing more impersonal and nebulous in proportion as the human mind is learning to understand natural phenomena and in the degree that science progressively correlates human and social events.

God, today, no longer represents the same forces as in the beginning of His existence; neither does He direct human destiny with the same Iron hand as of yore. Rather does the God idea express a sort of spiritualistic stimulus to satisfy the fads and fancies of every shade of human weakness. In the course of human development the God idea has been forced to adapt itself to every phase of human affairs, which is perfectly consistent with the origin of the idea itself.

The conception of gods originated in fear and curiosity. Primitive man, unable to understand the phenomena of nature and harassed by them, saw in every terrifying manifestation some sinister force expressly directed against him; and as ignorance and fear are the parents of all superstition, the troubled fancy of primitive man wove the God idea.

Very aptly, the world-renowned atheist and anarchist, Michael Bakunin, says in his great work God and the State: "All religions, with their gods, their demi-gods, and their prophets, their messiahs and their saints, were created by the prejudiced fancy of men who had not attained the full development and full possession of their faculties. Consequently, the religious heaven is nothing but the mirage in which man, exalted by ignorance and faith, discovered his own image, but enlarged and reversed — that is divinised. The history of religions, of the birth, grandeur, and the decline of the gods who had succeeded one another in human belief, is nothing, therefore, but the development of the collective intelligence and conscience of mankind. As fast as they discovered, in the course of their historically progressive advance, either in themselves or in external nature, a quality, or even any great defect whatever, they attributed it to their gods, after having exaggerated and enlarged it beyond measure, after the manner of children, by an act of their religious fancy... With all due respect, then, to the metaphysicians and religious idealists, philosophers, politicians or poets: the idea of God implies the abdication of human reason and justice; it is the most decisive negation of human liberty, and necessarily ends in the enslavement of mankind, both in theory and practice."

Thus the God idea, revived, readjusted, and enlarged or narrowed, according to the necessity of the time, has dominated humanity and will continue to do so until man will raise his head to the sunlit day, unafraid and with an awakened will to himself. In proportion as man learns to realize himself and mold his own destiny theism becomes superfluous. How far man will be able to find his relation to his fellows will depend entirely upon how much he can outgrow his dependence upon God.

Already there are indications that theism, which is the theory of speculation, is being replaced by Atheism, the science of demonstration; the one hangs in the metaphysical clouds of the Beyond, while the other has its roots firmly in the soil. It is the earth, not heaven, which man must rescue if he is truly to be saved.

The decline of theism is a most interesting spectacle, especially as manifested in the anxiety of the theists, whatever their particular brand. They realize, much to their distress, that the masses are growing daily more atheistic, more anti-religious; that they are quite willing to leave the Great Beyond and its heavenly domain to the angels and sparrows; because more and more the masses are becoming engrossed in the problems of their immediate existence.

How to bring the masses back to the God idea, the spirit, the First Cause, etc. — that is the most pressing question to all theists. Metaphysical as all these questions seem to be, they yet have a very marked physical background. Inasmuch as religion, "Divine Truth," rewards and punishments are the trade-marks of the largest, the most corrupt and pernicious, the most powerful and lucrative industry in the world, not excepting the industry of manufacturing guns and munitions. It is the industry of befogging the human mind and stifling the human heart. Necessity knows no law; hence the majority of theists are compelled to take up every subject, even if it has no bearing upon a deity or revelation or the Great Beyond. Perhaps they sense the fact that humanity is growing weary of the hundred and one brands of God.

How to raise this dead level of theistic belief is really a matter of life and death for all denominations. Therefore their tolerance; but it is a tolerance not of understanding; but of weakness. Perhaps that explains the efforts fostered in all religious publications to combine variegated religious philosophies and conflicting theistic theories into one denominational trust. More and more, the various concepts "of the only tree God, the only pure spirit, — the only true religion" are tolerantly glossed over in the frantic effort to establish a common ground to rescue the modern mass from the "pernicious" influence of atheistic ideas.

It is characteristic of theistic "tolerance" that no one really cares what the people believe in, just so they believe or pretend to believe. To accomplish this end, the crudest and vulgarest methods are being used. Religious endeavor meetings and revivals with Billy Sunday as their champion-methods which must outrage every refined sense, and which in their effect upon the ignorant and curious often tend to create a mild state of insanity not infrequently coupled with eroto-mania. All these frantic efforts find approval and support from the earthly powers; from the Russian despot to the American President; from Rockefeller and Wanamaker down to the pettiest business man. They blow that capital invested in Billy Sunday, the Y.M.C.A., Christian Science, and various other religious institutions will return enormous profits from the subdued, tamed, and dull masses.

Consciously or unconsciously, most theists see in gods and devils, heaven and hell; reward and punishment, a whip to lash the people into obedience, meekness and contentment. The truth is that theism would have lost its footing long before this but for the combined support of Mammon and power. How thoroughly bankrupt it really is, is being demonstrated in the trenches and battlefields of Europe today.

Have not all theists painted their Deity as the god of love and goodness? Yet after thousands of years of such preachments the gods remain deaf to the agony of the human race. Confucius cares not for the poverty, squalor and misery of people of China. Buddha remains undisturbed in his philosophical indifference to the famine and starvation of outraged Hindoos; Jahve continues deaf to the bitter cry of Israel; while Jesus refuses to rise from the dead against his Christians who are butchering each other.

The burden of all song and praise "unto the Highest" has been that God stands for justice and mercy. Yet injustice among men is ever on the increase; the outrages committed against the masses in this country alone would seem enough to overflow the very heavens. But where are the gods to make an end to all these horrors, these wrongs, this inhumanity to man? No, not the gods, but MAN must rise in his mighty wrath. He, deceived by all the deities, betrayed by their emissaries, he, himself, must undertake to usher in justice upon the earth.

The philosophy of Atheism expresses the expansion and growth of the human mind. The philosophy of theism, if we can call it philosophy, is static and fixed. Even the mere attempt to pierce these mysteries represents, from the theistic point of view, non-belief in the all-embracing omnipotence, and even a denial of the wisdom of the divine powers outside of man. Fortunately, however, the human mind never was, and never can be, bound by fixities. Hence it is forging ahead in its restless march towards knowledge and life. The human mind is realizing "that the universe is not the result of a creative fiat by some divine intelligence, out of nothing, producing a masterpiece chaotic in perfect operation," but that it is the product of chaotic forces operating through aeons of time, of clashes and cataclysms, of repulsion and attraction crystalizing through the principle of selection into what the theists call, "the universe guided into order and beauty." As Joseph McCabe well points out in his Existence of God: "a law of nature is not a formula drawn up by a legislator, but a mere summary of the observed facts — a 'bundle of facts.' Things do not act in a particular way because there is a law, but we state the 'law' because they act in that way."

The philosophy of Atheism represents a concept of life without any metaphysical Beyond or Divine Regulator. It is the concept of an actual, real world with its liberating, expanding and beautifying possibilities, as against an unreal world, which, with its spirits, oracles, and mean contentment has kept humanity in helpless degradation.

It may seem a wild paradox, and yet it is pathetically true, that this real, visible world and our life should have been so long under the influence of metaphysical speculation, rather than of physical demonstrable forces. Under the lash of the theistic idea, this earth has served no other purpose than as a temporary station to test man's capacity for immolation to the will of God. But the moment man attempted to ascertain the nature of that will, he was told that it was utterly futile for "finite human intelligence" to get beyond the all-powerful infinite will. Under the terrific weight of this omnipotence, man has been bowed into the dust — a will-less creature, broken and sweating in the dark. The triumph of the philosophy of Atheism is to free man from the nightmare of gods; it means the dissolution of the phantoms of the beyond. Again and again the light of reason has dispelled the theistic nightmare, but poverty, misery and fear have recreated the phantoms

— though whether old or new, whatever their external form, they differed little in their essence. Atheism, on the other hand, in its philosophic aspect refuses allegiance not merely to a definite concept of God, but it refuses all servitude to the God idea, and opposes the theistic principle as such. Gods in their individual function are not half as pernicious as the principle of theism which represents the belief in a supernatural, or even omnipotent, power to rule the earth and man upon it. It is the absolutism of theism, its pernicious influence upon humanity, its paralyzing effect upon thought and action, which Atheism is fighting with all its power.

The philosophy of Atheism has its root in the earth, in this life; its aim is the emancipation of the human race from all God-heads, be they Judaic, Christian, Mohammedan, Buddhistic, Brahministic, or what not. Mankind has been punished long and heavily for having created its gods; nothing but pain and persecution have been man's lot since gods began.

There is but one way out of this blunder: Man must break his fetters which have chained him to the gates of heaven and hell, so that he can begin to fashion out of his reawakened and illumined consciousness a new world upon earth.

Only after the triumph of the Atheistic philosophy in the minds and hearts of man will freedom and beauty be realized. Beauty as a gift from heaven has proved useless. It will, however, become the essence and impetus of life when man learns to see in the earth the only heaven fit for man. Atheism is already helping to free man from his dependence upon punishment and reward as the heavenly bargain-counter for the poor in spirit.

Do not all theists insist that there can be no morality, no justice, honesty or fidelity without the belief in a Divine Power? Based upon fear and hope, such morality has always been a vile product, imbued partly with self-righteousness, partly with hypocrisy. As to truth, justice, and fidelity, who have been their brave exponents and daring proclaimers? Nearly always the godless ones: the Atheists; they lived, fought, and died for them. They knew that justice, truth, and fidelity are not, conditioned in heaven, but that they are related to and interwoven with the tremendous changes going on in the social and material life of the human race; not fixed and eternal, but fluctuating, even as life itself. To what heights the philosophy of Atheism may yet attain, no one can prophesy. But this much can already be predicted: only by its regenerating fire will human relations be purged from the horrors of the past

Thoughtful people are beginning to realize that moral precepts, imposed upon humanity through religious terror, have become stereotyped and have therefore lost all vitality. A glance at life today, at its disintegrating character, its conflicting interests with their hatreds, crimes, and greed, suffices to prove the sterility of theistic morality.

Man must get back to himself before he can learn his relation to his fellows.

Prometheus chained to the Rock of Ages is doomed to remain the prey of the vultures of darkness. Unbind Prometheus, and you dispel the night and its horrors.

Atheism in its negation of gods is at the same time the strongest affirmation of man, and through man, the eternal yea to life, purpose, and beauty.

A New Declaration of Independence

When, in the course of human development, existing institutions prove inadequate to the needs of man, when they serve merely to enslave, rob, and oppress mankind, the people have the eternal right to rebel against, and overthrow, these institutions.

The mere fact that these forces — inimical to life, liberty, and the pursuit of happiness — are legalized by statute laws, sanctified by divine rights, and enforced by political power, in no way justifies their continued existence.

We hold these truths to be self-evident: that all human beings, irrespective of race, color, or sex, are born with the equal right to share at the table of life; that to secure this right, there must be established among men economic, social, and political freedom; we hold further that government exists but to maintain special privilege and property rights; that it coerces man into submission and therefore robs him of dignity, self-respect, and life.

The history of the American kings of capital and authority is the history of repeated crimes, injustice, oppression, outrage, and abuse, all aiming at the suppression of individual liberties and the exploitation of the people. A vast country, rich enough to supply all her children with all possible comforts, and insure well-being to all, is in the hands of a few, while the nameless millions are at the mercy of ruthless wealth gatherers, unscrupulous lawmakers, and corrupt politicians. Sturdy sons of America are forced to tramp the country in a fruitless search for bread, and many of her daughters are driven into the street, while thousands of tender children are daily sacrificed on the altar of Mammon. The reign of these kings is holding mankind in slavery, perpetuating poverty and disease, maintaining crime and corruption; it is fettering the spirit of liberty, throttling the voice of justice, and degrading and oppressing humanity. It is engaged in continual war and slaughter, devastating the country and destroying the best and finest qualities of man; it nurtures superstition and ignorance, sows prejudice and strife, and turns the human family into a camp of Ishmaelites.

We, therefore, the liberty-loving men and women, realizing the great injustice and brutality of this state of affairs, earnestly and boldly do hereby declare, That each and every individual is and ought to be free to own himself and to enjoy the full fruit of his labor; that man is absolved from all allegiance to the kings of authority and capital; that he has, by the very fact of his being, free access to the land and all means of production, and entire liberty of disposing of the fruits of his efforts; that each and every individual has the unquestionable and unabridgeable right of free and voluntary association with other equally sovereign individuals for economic, political, social, and all other purposes, and that to achieve this end man must emancipate himself from the sacredness of property, the respect for man-made law, the fear of the Church, the cowardice of public opinion, the stupid arrogance of national, racial, religious, and sex superiority, and from the narrow puritanical conception of human life. And for the support of this Declaration, and with a firm reliance on the harmonious blending of man's social and individual tendencies, the lovers of liberty joyfully consecrate their uncompromising devotion, their energy and intelligence, their solidarity and their lives.

This 'Declaration' was written at the request of a certain newspaper, which subsequently refused to publish it, though the article was already in composition.

Patriotism: A Menace to Liberty

What is patriotism? Is it love of one's birthplace, the place of childhood's recollections and hopes, dreams and aspirations? Is it the place where, in childlike naivety, we would watch the fleeting clouds, and wonder why we, too, could not run so swiftly? The place where we would count the milliard glittering stars, terror-stricken lest each one "an eye should be," piercing the very depths of our little souls? Is it the place where we would listen to the music of the birds, and long to have wings to fly, even as they, to distant lands? Or the place where we would sit at mother's knee, enraptured by wonderful tales of great deeds and conquests? In short, is it love for the spot, every inch representing dear and precious recollections of a happy, joyous, and playful childhood?

If that were patriotism, few American men of today could be called upon to be patriotic, since the place of play has been turned into factory, mill, and mine, while deafening sounds of machinery have replaced the music of the birds. Nor can we longer hear the tales of great deeds, for the stories our mothers tell today are but those of sorrow, tears, and grief.

What, then, is patriotism? "Patriotism, sir, is the last resort of scoundrels," said Dr. Johnson. Leo Tolstoy, the greatest anti-patriot of our times, defines patriotism as the principle that will justify the training of wholesale murderers; a trade that requires better equipment for the exercise of man-killing than the making of such necessities of life as shoes, clothing, and houses; a trade that guarantees better returns and greater glory than that of the average workingman.

Gustave Hervé, another great anti-patriot, justly calls patriotism a superstition — one far more injurious, brutal, and inhumane than religion. The superstition of religion originated in man's inability to explain natural phenomena. That is, when primitive man heard thunder or saw the lightning, he could not account for either, and therefore concluded that back of them must be a force greater than himself. Similarly he saw a supernatural force in the rain, and in the various other changes in nature. Patriotism, on the other hand, is a superstition artificially created and maintained through a network of lies and falsehoods; a superstition that robs man of his self-respect and dignity, and increases his arrogance and conceit.

Indeed, conceit, arrogance, and egotism are the essentials of patriotism. Let me illustrate. Patriotism assumes that our globe is divided into little spots, each one surrounded by an iron gate. Those who have had the fortune of being born on some particular spot, consider themselves better, nobler, grander, more intelligent than the living beings inhabiting any other spot. It is, therefore, the duty of everyone living on that chosen spot to fight, kill, and die in the attempt to impose his superiority upon all the others.

The inhabitants of the other spots reason in like manner, of course, with the result that, from early infancy, the mind of the child is poisoned with bloodcurdling stories about the Germans, the French, the Italians, Russians, etc. When the child has reached manhood, he is thoroughly saturated with the belief that he is chosen by the Lord himself to defend his country against the attack or invasion of any foreigner. It is for that purpose that we are clamoring for a greater army and navy, more battleships and ammunition. It is for that purpose that America has within a short time spent four hundred million dollars. Just think of it — four hundred million dollars taken from the produce of the people. For surely it is not the rich who contribute to patriotism. They are cosmopolitans, perfectly at home in every land. We in America know well the truth of this. Are not our rich Americans

Frenchmen in France, Germans in Germany, or Englishmen in England? And do they not squandor with cosmopolitan grace fortunes coined by American factory children and cotton slaves? Yes, theirs is the patriotism that will make it possible to send messages of condolence to a despot like the Russian Tsar, when any mishap befalls him, as President Roosevelt did in the name of his people, when Sergius was punished by the Russian revolutionists.

It is a patriotism that will assist the arch-murderer, Diaz, in destroying thousands of lives in Mexico, or that will even aid in arresting Mexican revolutionists on American soil and keep them incarcerated in American prisons, without the slightest cause or reason.

But, then, patriotism is not for those who represent wealth and power. It is good enough for the people. It reminds one of the historic wisdom of Frederick the Great, the bosom friend of Voltaire, who said: "Religion is a fraud, but it must be maintained for the masses."

That patriotism is rather a costly institution, no one will doubt after considering the following statistics. The progressive increase of the expenditures for the leading armies and navies of the world during the last quarter of a century is a fact of such gravity as to startle every thoughtful student of economic problems. It may be briefly indicated by dividing the time from 1881 to 1905 into five-year periods, and noting the disbursements of several great nations for army and navy purposes during the first and last of those periods. From the first to the last of the periods noted the expenditures of Great Britain increased from $2,101,848,936 to $4,143,226,885, those of France from $3,324,500,000 to $3,455,109,900, those of Germany from $725,000,200 to $2,700,375,600, those of the United States from $1,275,500,750 to $2,650,900,450, those of Russia from $1,900,975,500 to $5,250,445,100, those of Italy from $1,600,975,750 to $1,755,500,100, and those of Japan from $182,900,500 to $700,925,475.

The military expenditures of each of the nations mentioned increased in each of the five-year periods under review. During the entire interval from 1881 to 1905 Great Britain's outlay for her army increased fourfold, that of the United States was tripled, Russia's was doubled, that of Germany increased 35 per cent., that of France about 15 per cent., and that of Japan nearly 500 per cent. If we compare the expenditures of these nations upon their armies with their total expenditures for all the twenty-five years ending with 1905, the proportion rose as follows:

In Great Britain from 20 per cent. to 37; in the United States from 15 to 23; in France from 16 to 18; in Italy from 12 to 15; in Japan from 12 to 14. On the other hand, it is interesting to note that the proportion in Germany decreased from about 58 per cent. to 25, the decrease being due to the enormous increase in the imperial expenditures for other purposes, the fact being that the army expenditures for the period of 1901–5 were higher than for any five-year period preceding. Statistics show that the countries in which army expenditures are greatest, in proportion to the total national revenues, are Great Britain, the United States, Japan, France, and Italy, in the order named.

The showing as to the cost of great navies is equally impressive. During the twenty-five years ending with 1905 naval expenditures increased approximately as follows: Great Britain, 300 per cent.; France 60 per cent.; Germany 600 per cent.; the United States 525 per cent.; Russia 300 per cent.; Italy 250 per cent.; and Japan, 700 per cent. With the exception of Great Britain, the United States spends more for naval purposes than any other nation, and this expenditure bears also a larger proportion to the entire national disbursements than that of any other power. In the period 1881–5, the expenditure for the United States navy was $6.20 out of each $100 appropriated for all national purposes; the amount rose to $6.60 for the next five-year period, to $8.10 for the next, to $11.70 for the next, and to $16.40 for 1901–5. It is morally certain that the outlay for the current period of five years will show a still further increase.

The rising cost of militarism may be still further illustrated by computing it as a per capita tax on population. From the first to the last of the five-year periods taken as the basis for the comparisons here given, it has risen as follows: In Great Britain, from $18.47 to $52.50; in France, from $19.66 to $23.62; in Germany, from $10.17 to $15.51; in the United States, from $5.62 to $13.64; in Russia, from $6.14 to $8.37; in Italy, from $9.59 to $11.24, and in Japan from 86 cents to $3.11.

It is in connection with this rough estimate of cost per capita that the economic burden of militarism is most appreciable. The irresistible conclusion from available data is that the increase of expenditure for army and navy purposes is rapidly surpassing the growth of population in each of the countries considered in the present calculation. In other words, a continuation of the increased demands of militarism threatens each of those nations with a progressive exhaustion both of men and resources.

The awful waste that patriotism necessitates ought to be sufficient to cure the man of even average intelligence from this disease. Yet patriotism demands still more. The people are urged to be patriotic and for that luxury they pay, not only by supporting their "defenders," but even by sacrificing their own children. Patriotism requires allegiance to the flag, which means obedience and readiness to kill father, mother, brother, sister.

The usual contention is that we need a standing army to protect the country from foreign invasion. Every intelligent man and woman knows, however, that this is a myth maintained to frighten and coerce the foolish. The governments of the world, knowing each other's interests, do not invade each other. They have learned that they can gain much more by international arbitration of disputes than by war and conquest. Indeed, as Carlyle said, "War is a quarrel between two thieves too cowardly to fight their own battle; therefore they take boys from one village and another village, stick them into uniforms, equip them with guns, and let them loose like wild beasts against each other."

It does not require much wisdom to trace every war back to a similar cause. Let us take our own Spanish-American war, supposedly a great and patriotic event in the history of the United States. How our hearts burned with indignation against the atrocious Spaniards! True, our indignation did not flare up spontaneously. It was nurtured by months of newspaper agitation, and long after Butcher Weyler had killed off many noble Cubans and outraged many Cuban women. Still, in justice to the American Nation be it said, it did grow indignant and was willing to fight, and that it fought bravely. But when the smoke was over, the dead buried, and the cost of the war came back to the people in an increase in the price of commodities and rent — that is, when we sobered up from our patriotic spree it suddenly dawned on us that the cause of the Spanish-American war was the consideration of the price of sugar; or, to be more explicit, that the lives, blood, and money of the American people were used to protect the interests of American capitalists, which were threatened by the Spanish government. That this is not an exaggeration, but is based on absolute facts and figures, is best proven by the attitude of the American government to Cuban labor. When Cuba was firmly in the clutches of the United States, the very soldiers sent to liberate Cuba were ordered to shoot Cuban workingmen during the great cigarmakers' strike, which took place shortly after the war.

Nor do we stand alone in waging war for such causes. The curtain is beginning to be lifted on the motives of the terrible Russo-Japanese war, which cost so much blood and tears. And we see again that back of the fierce Moloch of war stands the still fiercer god of Commercialism. Kuropatkin, the Russian Minister of War during the Russo-Japanese struggle, has revealed the true secret behind the latter. The Tsar and his Grand Dukes, having invested money in Corean concessions, the war was forced for the sole purpose of speedily accumulating large fortunes.

The contention that a standing army and navy is the best security of peace is about as logical as the claim that the most peaceful citizen is he who goes about heavily armed. The experience of every-day life fully proves that the armed individual is invariably anxious to try his strength. The same is historically true of governments. Really peaceful countries do not waste life and energy in war preparations, with the result that peace is maintained.

However, the clamor for an increased army and navy is not due to any foreign danger. It is owing to the dread of the growing discontent of the masses and of the international spirit among the workers. It is to meet the internal enemy that the Powers of various countries are preparing themselves; an enemy, who, once awakened to consciousness, will prove more dangerous than any foreign invader.

The powers that have for centuries been engaged in enslaving the masses have made a thorough study of their psychology. They know that the people at large are like children whose despair, sorrow, and tears can be turned into joy with a little toy. And the more gorgeously the toy is dressed, the louder the colors, the more it will appeal to the million-headed child.

An army and navy represents the people's toys. To make them more attractive and acceptable, hundreds and thousands of dollars are being spent for the display of these toys. That was the purpose of the American government in equipping a fleet and sending it along the Pacific coast, that every American citizen should be made to feel the pride and glory of the United States. The city of San Francisco spent one hundred thousand dollars for the entertainment of the fleet; Los Angeles, sixty thousand; Seattle and Tacoma, about one hundred thousand. To entertain the fleet, did I say? To dine and wine a few superior officers, while the "brave boys" had to mutiny to get sufficient food. Yes, two hundred and sixty thousand dollars were spent on fireworks, theatre parties, and revelries, at a time when men, women, and children through the breadth and length of the country were starving in the streets; when thousands of unemployed were ready to sell their labor at any price.

Two hundred and sixty thousand dollars! What could not have been accomplished with such an enormous sum? But instead of bread and shelter, the children of those cities were taken to see the fleet, that it may remain, as one of the newspapers said, "a lasting memory for the child."

A wonderful thing to remember, is it not? The implements of civilized slaughter. If the mind of the child is to be poisoned with such memories, what hope is there for a true realization of human brotherhood?

We Americans claim to be a peace-loving people. We hate bloodshed; we are opposed to violence. Yet we go into spasms of joy over the possibility of projecting dynamite bombs from flying machines upon helpless citizens. We are ready to hang, electrocute, or lynch anyone, who, from economic necessity, will risk his own life in the attempt upon that of some industrial magnate. Yet our hearts swell with pride at the thought that America is becoming the most powerful nation on earth, and that it will eventually plant her iron foot on the necks of all other nations.

Such is the logic of patriotism.

Considering the evil results that patriotism is fraught with for the average man, it is as nothing compared with the insult and injury that patriotism heaps upon the soldier himself, — that poor, deluded victim of superstition and ignorance. He, the savior of his country, the protector of his nation, — what has patriotism in store for him? A life of slavish submission, vice, and perversion, during peace; a life of danger, exposure, and death, during war.

While on a recent lecture tour in San Francisco, I visited the Presidio, the most beautiful spot overlooking the Bay and Golden Gate Park. Its purpose should have been playgrounds for children, gardens and music for the recreation of the weary. Instead it is made ugly, dull, and gray by barracks, — barracks wherein the rich would not allow their dogs to dwell. In these miserable shanties soldiers are herded like cattle; here they waste their young days, polishing the boots and brass buttons of their superior officers. Here, too, I saw the distinction of classes: sturdy sons of a free Republic, drawn up in line like convicts, saluting every passing shrimp of a lieutenant. American equality, degrading manhood and elevating the uniform!

Barrack life further tends to develop tendencies of sexual perversion. It is gradually producing along this line results similar to European military conditions. Havelock Ellis, the noted writer on sex psychology, has made a thorough study of the subject. I quote: "Some of the barracks are great centers of male prostitution.... The number of soldiers who prostitute themselves is greater than we are willing to believe. It is no exaggeration to say that in certain regiments the presumption is in favor of the venality of the majority of the men.... On summer evenings Hyde Park and the neighborhood of Albert Gate are full of guardsmen and others plying a lively trade, and with little disguise, in uniform or out.... In most cases the proceeds form a comfortable addition to Tommy Atkins' pocket money."

To what extent this perversion has eaten its way into the army and navy can best be judged from the fact that special houses exist for this form of prostitution. The practice is not limited to England; it is universal. "Soldiers are no less sought after in France than in England or in Germany, and special houses for military prostitution exist both in Paris and the garrison towns."

Had Mr. Havelock Ellis included America in his investigation of sex perversion, he would have found that the same conditions prevail in our army and navy as in those of other countries. The growth of the standing army inevitably adds to the spread of sex perversion; the barracks are the incubators.

Aside from the sexual effects of barrack life, it also tends to unfit the soldier for useful labor after leaving the army. Men, skilled in a trade, seldom enter the army or navy, but even they, after a military experience, find themselves totally unfitted for their former occupations. Having acquired habits of idleness and a taste for excitement and adventure, no peaceful pursuit can content them. Released from the army, they can turn to no useful work. But it is usually the social riff-raff, discharged prisoners and the like, whom either the struggle for life or their own inclination drives into the ranks. These, their military term over, again turn to their former life of crime, more brutalized and degraded than before. It is a well-known fact that in our prisons there is a goodly number of ex-soldiers; while, on the other hand, the army and navy are to a great extent plied with ex-convicts.

Of all the evil results I have just described none seems to me so detrimental to human integrity as the spirit patriotism has produced in the case of Private William Buwalda. Because he foolishly believed that one can be a soldier and exercise his rights as a man at the same time, the military authorities punished him severely. True, he had served his country fifteen years, during which time his record was unimpeachable. According to Gen. Funston, who reduced Buwalda's sentence to three years, "the first duty of an officer or an enlisted man is unquestioned obedience and loyalty to the government, and it makes no difference whether he approves of that government or not." Thus Funston stamps the true character of allegiance. According to him, entrance into the army abrogates the principles of the Declaration of Independence.

What a strange development of patriotism that turns a thinking being into a loyal machine!

In justification of this most outrageous sentence of Buwalda, Gen. Funston tells the American people that the soldier's action was "a serious crime equal to treason." Now, what did this "terrible crime" really consist of? Simply in this: William Buwalda was one of fifteen hundred people who attended a public meeting in San Francisco; and, oh, horrors, he shook hands with the speaker, Emma Goldman. A terrible crime, indeed, which the General calls "a great military offense, infinitely worse than desertion."

Can there be a greater indictment against patriotism than that it will thus brand a man a criminal, throw him into prison, and rob him of the results of fifteen years of faithful service?

Buwalda gave to his country the best years of his life and his very manhood. But all that was as nothing. Patriotism is inexorable and, like all insatiable monsters, demands all or nothing. It does not admit that a soldier is also a human being, who has a right to his own feelings and opinions, his own inclinations and ideas. No, patriotism can not admit of that. That is the lesson which Buwalda was made to learn; made to learn at a rather costly, though not at a useless price. When he returned to freedom, he had lost his position in the army, but he regained his self-respect. After all, that is worth three years of imprisonment.

A writer on the military conditions of America, in a recent article, commented on the power of the military man over the civilian in Germany. He said, among other things, that if our Republic had no other meaning than to guarantee all citizens equal rights, it would have just cause for existence. I am convinced that the writer was not in Colorado during the patriotic régime of General Bell. He probably would have changed his mind had he seen how, in the name of patriotism and the Republic, men were thrown into bull-pens, dragged about, driven across the border, and subjected to all kinds of indignities. Nor is that Colorado incident the only one in the growth of military power in the United States. There is hardly a strike where troops and militia do not come to the rescue of those in power, and where they do not act as arrogantly and brutally as do the men wearing the Kaiser's uniform. Then, too, we have the Dick military law. Had the writer forgotten that?

A great misfortune with most of our writers is that they are absolutely ignorant on current events, or that, lacking honesty, they will not speak of these matters. And so it has come to pass that the Dick military law was rushed through Congress with little discussion and still less publicity, — a law which gives the President the power to turn a peaceful citizen into a bloodthirsty man-killer, supposedly for the defense of the country, in reality for the protection of the interests of that particular party whose mouthpiece the President happens to be.

Our writer claims that militarism can never become such a power in America as abroad, since it is voluntary with us, while compulsory in the Old World. Two very important facts, however, the gentleman forgets to consider. First, that conscription has created in Europe a deep-seated hatred of militarism among all classes of society. Thousands of young recruits enlist under protest and, once in the army, they will use every possible means to desert. Second, that it is the compulsory feature of militarism which has created a tremendous anti-militarist movement, feared by European Powers far more than anything else. After all, the greatest bulwark of capitalism is militarism. The very moment the latter is undermined, capitalism will totter. True, we have no conscription; that is, men are not usually forced to enlist in the army, but we have developed a far more exacting and rigid force — necessity. Is it not a fact that during industrial depressions there is a tremendous increase in the number of enlistments? The trade of militarism may not be either lucrative or honorable, but it is better than tramping the country in search of work, standing in the bread line, or sleeping in municipal lodging houses. After all, it means thirteen dollars per month, three meals a day, and a place to sleep. Yet even necessity is not sufficiently strong a factor to bring into the army an element of character and manhood. No wonder our military authorities complain of the "poor material" enlisting in the army and navy. This admission is a very encouraging sign. It proves that there is still enough of the spirit of independence and love of liberty left in the average American to risk starvation rather than don the uniform.

Thinking men and women the world over are beginning to realize that patriotism is too narrow and limited a conception to meet the necessities of our time. The centralization of power has brought into being an international feeling of solidarity among the oppressed nations of the world; a solidarity which represents a greater harmony of interests between the workingman of America and his brothers abroad than between the American miner and his exploiting compatriot; a solidarity which fears not foreign invasion, because it is bringing all the workers to the point when they will say to their masters, "Go and do your own killing. We have done it long enough for you."

This solidarity is awakening the consciousness of even the soldiers, they, too, being flesh of the flesh of the great human family. A solidarity that has proven infallible more than once during past struggles, and which has been the impetus inducing the Parisian soldiers, during the Commune of 1871, to refuse to obey when ordered to shoot their brothers. It has given courage to the men who mutinied on Russian warships during recent years. It will eventually bring about the uprising of all the oppressed and downtrodden against their international exploiters.

The proletariat of Europe has realized the great force of that solidarity and has, as a result, inaugurated a war against patriotism and its bloody spectre, militarism. Thousands of men fill the prisons of France, Germany, Russia, and the Scandinavian countries, because they dared to defy the ancient superstition. Nor is the movement limited to the working class; it has embraced representatives in all stations of life, its chief exponents being men and women prominent in art, science, and letters.

America will have to follow suit. The spirit of militarism has already permeated all walks of life. Indeed, I am convinced that militarism is growing a greater danger here than anywhere else, because of the many bribes capitalism holds out to those whom it wishes to destroy.

The beginning has already been made in the schools. Evidently the government holds to the Jesuitical conception, "Give me the child mind, and I will mould the man." Children are trained in military tactics, the glory of military achievements extolled in the curriculum, and the youthful minds perverted to suit the government. Further, the youth of the country is appealed to in glaring posters to join the army and navy. "A fine chance to see the world!" cries the governmental huckster. Thus innocent boys are morally shanghaied into patriotism, and the military Moloch strides conquering through the Nation.

The American workingman has suffered so much at the hands of the soldier, State and Federal, that he is quite justified in his disgust with, and his opposition to, the uniformed parasite. However, mere denunciation will not solve this great problem. What we need is a propaganda of education for the soldier: antipatriotic literature that will enlighten him as to the real horrors of his trade, and that will awaken his consciousness to his true relation to the man to whose labor he owes his very existence.

It is precisely this that the authorities fear most. It is already high treason for a soldier to attend a radical meeting. No doubt they will also stamp it high treason for a soldier to read a radical pamphlet. But, then, has not authority from time immemorial stamped every step of progress as treasonable? Those, however, who earnestly strive for social reconstruction can well afford to face all that; for it is probably even more important to carry the truth into the barracks than into the factory. When we have undermined the patriotic lie, we shall have cleared the path for that great structure wherein all nationalities shall be united into a universal brotherhood, — a truly FREE SOCIETY.

The Social Aspects of Birth Control

It has been suggested that to create one genius nature uses all of her resources and takes a hundred years for her difficult task. If that be true, it takes nature even longer to create a great idea. After all, in creating a genius nature concentrates on one personality whereas an idea must eventually become the heritage of the race and must needs be more difficult to mould.

It is just one hundred and fifty years ago when a great man conceived a great idea, Robert Thomas Malthus, the father of Birth Control. That it should have taken so long a time for the human race to realize the greatness of that idea, is only one more proof of the sluggishness of the human mind. It is not possible to go into a detailed discussion of the merits of Malthus' contention, to wit, that the earth is not fertile or rich enough to supply the needs of an excessive race. Certainly if we will look across to the trenches and battlefields of Europe we will find that in a measure his premise was correct. But I feel confident that if Malthus would live to-day he would agree with all social students and revolutionists that if the masses of people continue to be poor and the rich grow ever richer, it is not because the earth is lacking in fertility and richness to supply the need even of an excessive race, but because the earth is monopolized in the hands of the few to the exclusion of the many.

Capitalism, which was in its baby's shoes during Malthus' time has since grown into a huge insatiable monster. It roars through its whistle and machine, "Send your children on to me, I will twist their bones; I will sap their blood, I will rob them of their bloom," for capitalism has an insatiable appetite.

And through its destructive machinery, militarism, capitalism proclaims, "Send your sons on to me, I will drill and discipline them until all humanity has been ground out of them; until they become automatons ready to shoot and kill at the behest of their masters." Capitalism cannot do without militarism and since the masses of people furnish the material to be destroyed in the trenches and on the battlefield, capitalism must have a large race.

In so called good times, capitalism swallows masses of people to throw them out again in times of "industrial depression." This superfluous human mass, which is swelling the ranks of the unemployed and which represents the greatest menace in modern times, is called by our bourgeois political economists the labor margin. They will have it that under no circumstances must the labor margin diminish, else the sacred institution known as capitalistic civilization will be undermined. And so the political economists, together with all sponsors of the capitalistic regime, are in favor of a large and excessive race and are therefore opposed to Birth Control.

Nevertheless Malthus' theory contains much more truth than fiction. In its modern aspect it rests no longer upon speculation, but on other factors which are related to and interwoven with the tremendous social changes going on everywhere.

First, there is the scientific aspect, the contention on the part of the most eminent men of science who tell us that an overworked and underfed vitality cannot reproduce healthy progeny. Beside the contention of scientists, we are confronted with the terrible fact which is now even recognized by benighted people, namely, that an indiscriminate and incessant breeding on the part of the over-worked and underfed masses has resulted in an increase of defective, crippled and unfortunate children. So alarming is this fact, that it has awakened social reformers to the necessity of a mental clearing house where the cause and effect of the increase of crippled, deaf, dumb and blind children may be ascertained. Knowing as we do that reformers accept the truth when it has become apparent to the dullest in society, there need be no discussion any longer in regard to the results of indiscriminate breeding.

Secondly, there is the mental awakening of woman, that plays no small part in behalf of Birth Control. For ages she has carried her burdens. Has done her duty a thousand fold more than the soldier on the battlefield. After all, the soldier's business is to take life. For that he is paid by the State, eulogized by political charlatans and upheld by public hysteria. But woman's function is to give life, yet neither the state nor politicians nor public opinion have ever made the slightest provision in return for the life woman has given.

For ages she has been on her knees before the altar of duty as imposed by God, by Capitalism, by the State, and by Morality. To-day she has awakened from her age-long sleep. She has shaken herself free from the nightmare of the past; she has turned her face towards the light and its proclaiming in a clarion voice that she will no longer be a party to the crime of bringing hapless children into the world only to be ground into dust by the wheel of capitalism and to be torn into shreds in trenches and battlefields. And who is to say her nay? After all it is woman who is risking her health and sacrificing her youth in the reproduction of the race. Surely she ought to be in a position to decide how many children she should bring into the world, whether they should be brought into the world by the man she loves and because she wants the child, or should be born in hatred and loathing.

Furthermore, it is conceded by earnest physicians that constant reproduction on the part of women has resulted in what the laity terms, "female troubles": a lucrative condition for unscrupulous medical men. But what possible reason has woman to exhaust her system in ever-lasting child bearing?

It is precisely for this reason that women should have the knowledge that would enable her to recuperate during a period of from three to five years between each pregnancy, which alone would give her physical and mental well-being and the opportunity to take better care of the children already in existence.

But it is not woman alone who is beginning to realize the importance of Birth Control. Men, too, especially working men, have learned to see in large families a millstone around their necks, deliberately imposed upon them by the reactionary forces in society because a large family paralyzes the brain and benumbs the muscles of the masses of working men. Nothing so binds the workers to the block as a brood of children and that is exactly what the opponents of Birth Control want. Wretched as the earnings of a man with a large family are, he cannot risk even that little, so he continues in the rut, compromises and cringes before his master, just to earn barely enough to feed the many little mouths. He dare not join a revolutionary organization; he dare not go on strike; he dare not express an opinion. Masses of workers have awakened to the necessity of Birth Control as a means of freeing themselves from the terrible yoke and still more as a means of being able to do something for those already in existence by preventing more children from coming into the world.

Last, but not least, a change in the relation of the sexes, though not embracing very large numbers of people, is still making itself felt among a very considerable minority. In the past and to a large extent with the average man to-day. woman continues to be a mere object, a means to an end; largely a physical means and end. But there are men who want more than that from woman; who have come to realize that if every male were emancipated from the superstitions of the past nothing would yet be changed in the social structure so long as woman had not taken her place with him in the great social struggle. Slowly but surely these men have learned that if a woman wastes her substance in eternal pregnancies, confinements and diaper washing, she has little time left for anything else. Least of all has she time for the questions which absorb and stir the father of her children. Out of physical exhaustion and nervous stress she becomes the obstacle in the man's way and often his bitterest enemy. It is then for his own protection and also for his need of the companion and friend in the woman he loves that a great many men want her to be relieved from the terrible imposition of constant reproduction of life, that therefore they are in favor of Birth Control.

From whatever angle, then, the question of Birth Control may be considered, it is the most dominant issue of modern times and as such it cannot be driven back by persecution, imprisonment or a conspiracy of silence.

Those who oppose the Birth Control

Movement claim to do so in behalf of motherhood. All the political charlatans prate about this wonderful motherhood, yet on closer examination we find that this motherhood has gone on for centuries past blindly and stupidly dedicating its offspring to Moloch. Besides, so long as mothers are compelled to work many hard hours in order to help support the creatures which they unwillingly brought into the world, the talk of motherhood is nothing else but cant. Ten per cent, of married women in the city of New York have to help make a living. Most of them earn the very lucrative salary of $280 a year. How dare anyone speak of the beauties of Motherhood in the face of such a crime?

But even the better paid mothers, what of them? Not so long ago our old and hoary Board of Education declared that mother teachers may not continue to teach. Though these antiquated gentlemen were compelled by public opinion to reconsider their decision, it is absolutely certain that if the average teacher were to become a mother every year, she would soon lose her position. This is the lot of the married mother; what about the unmarried mother? Or is anyone in doubt that there are thousands of unmarried mothers? They crowd our shops and factories and industries everywhere, not by choice but by economic necessity. In their drab and monotonous existence the only color left is probably a sexual attraction which without methods of prevention invariably leads to abortions. Thousands of women are sacrificed as a result of abortions because they are undertaken by quack doctors, ignorant midwives in secrecy and in haste. Yet the poets and the politicians sing of motherhood. A greater crime was never perpetrated upon woman.

Our moralists know about it, yet they persist in behalf of an indiscriminate breeding of children. They tell us that to limit offspring is entirely a modern tendency because the modern woman is loose in her morals and wishes to shirk responsibility. In reply to this, it is necessary to point out that the tendency to limit offspring is as old as the race. We have as the authority for this contention an eminent German physician Dr. Theilhaber who has compiled historic data to prove that the tendency was prevalent among the Hebrews, the Egyptians, the Persians and many tribes of American Indians. The fear of the child was so great that the women used the most hideous methods rather than to bring an unwanted child into the world. Dr. Theilhaber enumerates fifty-seven methods. This data is of great importance in as much as it dispels the superstition that woman wants to become a mother of a large family.

No, it is not because woman is lacking in responsibility, but because she has too much of the latter that she demands to know how to prevent conception. Never in the history of the world has woman been so race conscious as she is to-day. Never before has she been able to see in the child, not only in her child, but every child, the unit of society, the channel through which man and woman must pass; the strongest factor in the building of a new world. It is for this reason that Birth Control rests upon such solid ground.

We are told that so long as the law on the statute books makes the discussion of preventives a crime, these preventives must not be discussed. In reply I wish to say that it is not the Birth Control Movement, but the law, which will have to go. After all, that is what laws are for, to be made and unmade. How dare they demand that life shall submit to them? Just because some ignorant bigot in his own limitation of mind and heart succeeded in passing a law at the time when men and women were in the thralls of religious and moral superstition, must we be bound by it for the rest of our lives? I readily understand why judges and jailers shall be bound by it. It means their livelihood; their function in society. But even judges sometimes progress. I call your attention to the decision given in behalf of the issue of Birth Control by Judge Gatens of Portland, Oregon. "It seems to me that the trouble with our people to-day is, that there is too much prudery. Ignorance and prudery have always been the millstones around the neck of progress. We all know that things are wrong in society; that we are suffering from many evils but we have not the nerve to get up and admit it, and when some person brings to our attention something we already know, we feign modesty and feel outraged." That certainly is the trouble with most of our law makers and with all those who are opposed to Birth Control.

I am to be tried at Special Sessions April 5th. I do not know what the outcome will be, and furthermore, I do not care. This dread of going to prison for one's ideas so prevalent among American radicals, is what makes the movement so pale and weak. I have no such dread. My revolutionary tradition is that those who are not willing to go to prison for their ideas have never been considered of much value to their ideas. Besides, there are worse places than prison. But whether I have to pay for my Birth Control activities or come out free, one thing is certain, the Birth Control movement cannot be stopped nor will I be stopped from carrying on Birth Control agitation. If I refrain from discussing methods, it is not because I am afraid of a second arrest, but because for the first time in the history of America, the issue of Birth Control through oral information is clear-cut and as I want it fought out on its merits, I do not wish to give the authorities an opportunity to obscure it by something else. However, I do want to point out the utter stupidity of the law. I have at hand the testimony given by the detectives, which, according to their statement, is an exact transcription of what I spelled for them from the platform. Yet so ignorant are these men that they have not a single contracept spelled correctly now. It is perfectly within the law for the detectives to give testimony, but it is not within the law for me to read the testimony which resulted in my indictment. Can you blame me if I am an anarchist and have no use for laws? Also, I wish to point out the utter stupidity of the American court. Supposedly justice is to be meted out there. Supposedly there are to be no star chamber proceedings under democracy, yet the other day when the detectives gave their testimony, it had to be done in a whisper, close to the judge as at the confessional in a Catholic Church and under no circumstances were the ladies present permitted to hear anything that was going on. The farce of it all! And yet we are expected to respect it, to obey it, to submit to it.

I do not know how many of you are willing to do it, but I am not. I stand as one of the sponsors of a world-wide movement, a movement which aims to set woman free from the terrible yoke and bondage of enforced pregnancy; a movement which demands the right for every child to be well born; a movement which shall help free labor from its eternal dependence; a movement which shall usher into the world a new kind of motherhood. I consider this movement important and vital enough to defy all the laws upon the statute-books. I believe it will clear the way not merely for the free discussion of contracepts but for the freedom of expression in Life, Art and Labor, for the right of medical science to experiment with contracepts as it has in the treatment of tuberculosis or any other disease.

I may be arrested, I may be tried and thrown into jail, but I never will be silent; I never will acquiesce or submit to authority, nor will I make peace with a system which degrades woman to a mere incubator and which fattens on her innocent victims. I now and here declare war upon this system and shall not rest until the path has been cleared for a free motherhood and a healthy, joyous and happy childhood.

Political Persecution in Republican Spain

On my first visit to Spain in September 1936, nothing surprised me so much as the amount of political freedom I found everywhere. True it did not extend to fascists; but outside of these deliberate enemies of the revolution and the emancipation of the workers in Spain, everyone of the anti-fascist front enjoyed political freedom which hardly existed in any of the so called European democracies. The one party that made the utmost use of this was the PSUC, the Stalinist party in revolutionary Spain. Their radio and loudspeakers filled the air. Their daily marches in military formation with their flags waving were flaunted in everybody's face. They seemed to take a special pleasure in marching past the house of the Regional

Committee as if they wanted to make the CNT-FAI aware of their determination to strike the blow when they will attain to complete power. This was obvious to anyone among the foreign delegates and comrades who had come to help in the anti-fascist struggle. Not so our Spanish comrades. They made light of the communist brazenness. They insisted that this circus clap trap could not decide the revolutionary struggle, and that they themselves had more important things to do than waste their time in idle display. It seemed to me that the Spanish comrades had little understanding of mass psychology which needs flagwagging, speeches, music and demonstrations — that while the CNT-FAI however, were concentrated on their constructive tasks, and fighting on the various fronts, their communist allies made hay while their sun shone. They have since proved that they knew what they were about.

During my stay of three months I visited many of the collectivised estates and factories, maternities and hospitals in Barcelona, and last but not least, also the 'Modelo' prison. Then the place that had harboured some of the most distinguished revolutionaries and anarchists of Catalonia. Our own heroic comrades Durruti and Ascaso, Garcia Oliver and many others had been cell neighbours of Companys, the new President of the Generalitat. I visited this institution in the presence of a comrade, a physician who had made a special study of criminal psychology The director gave me free access to every part of the prison and the right to speak to any of the fascists without the presence of guards. Among the few hundred admirers of Franco were officers and priests. They assured me in one voice of the decent and just treatment they were receiving from the management in charge of the place, most of whom were CNT-FAI men.

The possibility that fascists would soon be replaced by revolutionists and anarchists was far removed from my mind. If anything, the high water mark of the revolution in the autumn of 1936 held out hopes that the stain of prison would be wiped out once Franco and his hordes were defeated.

The report of the foul murder of the most gentle of anarchists, Camillo Berneri and his room mate, the anarchist Barbieri, was followed by wholesale arrests, mutilation and death. They seemed too fantastic, the change in the internal political situation too incredible to be true. I decided to go back to Spain to see for myself how far the new found freedom of the Spanish masses had been annihilated by Stalin's henchmen.

Once again I arrived on the 16th September this year. I went straight to Valencia and there discovered that 1,500 CNT members, comrades of the FAI and the Libertarian Youth hundreds of the POUM and even members of the International Brigade were filling the prisons of Valencia. During my short stay there I left no stone unturned to get permission to visit some of our comrades, among them Gustel Dorster whom I had known in Germany as most active in the anarcho-syndicalist movements before Hitler ascended to power. I was assured that I would be given permission; but at the last moment, before my return to Barcelona, I was informed that foreigners were not allowed to see the prison. I soon discovered the same situation repeated in every town and village I visited. Thousands of comrades and other genuine revolutionaries were filling the prisons under the Negrin-Prieto and Stalinist regime.

When I came back to Barcelona in the early part of October, I immediately sought to see our comrades in the Modelo prison. After many difficulties comrade Augustin Souchy succeeded in obtaining permission to have an interview with a few of the German comrades. Much to my surprise I found on my arrival there that the same Director was still in charge. He too recognised me and he again gave me full entry to the prison. I did not need to speak to the comrades through the hideous bars. I was in the hall where they foregather, surrounded by German, Italian, Bulgarian, Russian and Spanish comrades, all trying to speak at once and tell me of their conditions. I discovered no charge whatever that would stand in any Court, even under capitalism, had been prefered against them, except the idiotic charge of 'Trotskyism'.

These men from every part of the globe had flocked to Spain, often begging their way across, to help the Spanish revolution, to join the ranks of the anti-fascists and to lay down their lives in the struggle against Franco were held captive. Others again had been picked up on the street and had vanished without leaving any trace behind. Among the many was Reis, son of the internationally known Russian Menshevik Abramovich.

The most recent victim is Kurt Landau, a former member of the Executive Committee of the Austrian Communist Party, and before his arrest on the Executive Committee of the POUM Every effort to find him has met with failure. In view of the disappearance of Andres Nin of the POUM and scores of others it is reasonable to conclude that Kurt Landau met with the same fate.

But to return to the Modelo prison. It is impossible to give all the names, because there are so many incarcerated there. The most outstanding is a comrade who, in a high responsible position before the May events, had turned over millions of pesetas to the Generalitat found in Churches and Palaces. He is held under the ludicrous charge of having embezzled 100,000 pesetas.

Another one is comrade Helmut Klose, a member of the CNT-FAI. He was arrested on the 2nd July. No charge has been made up to this date, neither was he brought before a Judge. Comrade Klose was a member of the FAUD in Germany (German anarcho-syndicalist organisation). After having been arrested several times, he emigrated to Yugoslavia in the summer of 1933. Expelled from there in

February 1937, because of anti-fascist activity. He came to Spain in March. He joined the frontier service of the FAI, in the 'De la Costa' battalion. After the dissolution of this battalion, in June he took his discharge, entered the service of the agricultural collective in San Anores. In compliance with the request from his group he undertook the reorganisation of the Tailors' Collective of the Emigrants Committee. The charge made by the Cheka of his having disarmed officers while in the Frontier Service at Figueras is entirely without foundation.

Commander de Alkert Kille. He was arrested on September 7th. No reason was given. In Germany he had belonged since 1919 to the Productive Supply Union. Besides this he was a member of the Communist Party. In 1933 he emigrated to Austria. After the February events he fled to Prague: but later returned to Austria whence he was expelled and left for France. Here he joined the German anarcho-syndicalist group. In August 1936 he went to Spain, where he at once proceeded to the front. He was wounded once. He belonged to the Durruti column right up to the time of the militarisation. In June he took his discharge.

I also visited the POUM Sector. Many of these prisoners are Spaniards, but amongst them there are also a large number foreigners, Italian, French, Russian and German. Two members of the POUM approached me personally. They said little of their own suffering, but begged me to take a message to their own wives in Paris. They were Nicolas Sundelevich — the son of the famous Menshevik who had spent the longest part of his life in Siberia. Nicolas Sundelevich certainly did not give me the impression being guilty of the serious charges made against him of 'having given the fascists information' among the many other charges against him. It takes the perverted communist mind to hold a man in prison because in 1922 he had illegally left Russia.

Richard Tietz was arrested as he came

out of the Argentine Consulate in Barcelona where he had gone on behalf of his wife, previously arrested. When he demanded to know the grounds his arrest the Commissar nonchalantly said "I consider it just". That was evidently enough to keep Richard Tietz in the Modelo since July.

As far as prison conditions can be humane the Modelo is certainly superior to the Cheka prisons introduced in Spain by the Stalinists according to the best party examples of Soviet Russia. The 'Modelo' still maintains its traditional political privileges such as the right of the inmates to freely mingle together, organise their committees to represent them with the director, receiving parcels, tobacco, etc., in addition to the scanty prison fare. They can also write and receive letters and reading material. Besides, the prisoners issue little prison papers and bulletins which they can paste in the corridors where they all foregather. Both in the section of our comrades and the POUM I found such prison papers, posters and photographs of the heroes of the two parties. The POUM had even a very fine drawing of Andres Nin and a picture of Rosa Luxemburg, while the anarchist's side had Ascaso and Durruti on their wall.

Most interesting was the Durruti cell which he had occupied in Barcelona until released by the 1936 elections. It was left intact as it had been while Durruti was its involuntary lodger. Several large posters of our gallant comrade made the cell very much alive. The strangest part is however that the Durruti cell is in the fascist section. In answer to my question as to how Durruti's cell comes to be in there, I was told by the guard, "as an example of the living spirit of Durruti that will destroy fascism". I wanted very much to have the Durruti cell photographed but permission had to be obtained from the Minister of Justice. I gave up the idea. I had never in my life asked favours of Ministers of Justice, much less would I ask for anything from the counter-revolutionary government, the Spanish Cheka.

My next visit was to the womens' prison, which I found better kept and more cheerful than the Modelo. Only six women politicals were there at the time. Among them Katia Landau the wife of Kurt Landau, who had been arrested several months before him. She was like the old time Russian revolutionists utterly devoted to her ideas. I already knew of her husband's disappearance and possible end; but I did not have the heart to disclose this fact to her. This was in October. In November I was informed by some of her comrades in Paris that Mrs Landau had begun a hunger strike on the 11th November. I have just received word that as a result of two hunger strikes Katia Landau has been released.

A few days before my departure from Spain I was informed on good authority that the old dreadful Bastille — Montjuich was again being used to house political prisoners. The infamous Montjuich, whose every stone could tell of man's inhumanity to man, of the thousands put to death by the most savage methods of torture, or driven mad or to suicide. Montjuich where in 1897 the Spanish Inquisition had been reintroduced by Canova Del Castillo, then Premier of Spain. It was at his behest that 30 workers, among them distinguished Spanish anarchists, had been kept for months in underground damp and dirty cells — repeatedly tortured and denied counsel. It was in Montjuich that Francisco Ferrer was murdered by the Spanish Government and the Catholic Church. Last year I visited this terrifying fortress. Then it held no prisoners. The cells were empty. We descended into black depths with torches guiding our way. I almost seemed to hear the agonised cries of the thousands of victims who had breathed their last in the ghastly holes. It was a relief to get into the light again.

History does repeat itself after all. Montjuich again serves its old ghastly purpose. It is overcrowded with ardent revolutionaries who had been among the first to rush to the various fronts. Militiants of the Durruti column freely giving their health and strength but unwilling to be turned into military automatons — members of the International Brigade who had come to Spain from every land to fight fascism, only to discover the harsh differentiation against them, their officers and the political commissars and the criminal waste of human lives due to the military ignorance and for party purpose and glory. All these and more are incarcerated in the fortress of Montjuich.

Since the world slaughter and the continued horror under dictatorship, red and black, human sensibilities have been atrophied; but there must be a few left who still have a sense of justice. True Anatole France, Georg Brandes and so many great souls whose protests saved twenty two victims of the Soviet State in 1922 are no longer with us. Still there are the Gides, the Silones, Aldous Huxley, Havelock Ellis, John Cowper Powys, Rebecca West, Ethel Mannin and others who would surely protest if made aware of the political persecutions rampant under the Negrin Prieto and Communist regime.

At any rate I cannot be silent in the face of such barbarous political persecutions. In justice to the thousands of our comrades in prison I have left behind. I will, and must, speak out.

Anarchy & the Sex Question

The workingman, whose strength and muscles are so admired by the pale, puny off-springs of the rich, yet whose labour barely brings him enough to keep the wolf of starvation from the door, marries only to have a wife and house-keeper, who must slave from morning till night, who must make every effort to keep down expenses. Her nerves are so tired by the continual effort to make the pitiful wages of her husband support both of them that she grows irritable and no longer is successful in concealing her want of affection for her lord and master, who, alas! soon comes to the conclusion that his hopes and plans have gone astray, and so practically begins to think that marriage is a failure.

The Chain Grows Heavier and Heavier

As the expenses grow larger instead of smaller, the wife, who has lost all of the little strength she had at marriage, likewise feels herself betrayed, and the constant fretting and dread of starvation consumes her beauty in a short time after marriage. She grows despondent, neglects her household duties, and as there are no ties of love and sympathy between herself and her husband to give them strength to face the misery and poverty of their lives, instead of clinging to each other, they become more and more estranged, more and more impatient with each other's faults.

The man cannot, like the millionaire, go to his club, but he goes to a saloon and tries to drown his misery in a glass of beer or whiskey. The unfortunate partner of his misery, who is too honest to seek forgetfulness in the arms of a lover, and who is too poor to allow herself any legitimate recreation or amusement, remains amid the squalid, half-kept surroundings she calls home, and bitterly bemoans the folly that made her a poor man's wife.

Yet there is no way for them to part from each other.

But They Must Wear It

However galling the chain which has been put around their necks by the law and Church may be, it may not be broken unless those two persons decide to permit it to be severed.

Should the law be merciful enough to grant them liberty, every detail of their private life must be dragged to light. The woman is condemned by public opinion and her whole life is ruined. The fear of this disgrace often causes her to break down under the heavy weight of married life without daring to enter a single protest against the outrageous system that has crushed her and so many of her sisters.

The rich endure it to avoid scandal — the poor for the sake of their children and the fear of public opinion. Their lives are one long continuation of hypocrisy and deceit.

The woman who sells her favours is at liberty to leave the man who purchases them at any time, "while the respectable wife" cannot free herself from a union which is galling to her.

All unnatural unions which are not hallowed by love are prostitution, whether sanctioned by the Church and society or not. Such unions cannot have other than a degrading influence both upon the morals and health of society.

The System is to Blame

The system which forces women to sell their womanhood and independence to the highest bidder is a branch of the same evil system which gives to a few the right to live on the wealth produced by their fellow-men, 99 percent of whom must toil and slave early and late for barely enough to keep soul and body together, while the fruits of their labour are absorbed by a few idle vampires who are surrounded by every luxury wealth can purchase.

Look for a moment at two pictures of this nineteenth century social system.

Look at the homes of the wealthy, those magnificent palaces whose costly furnishings would put thousands of needy men and women in comfortable circumstances. Look at the dinner parties of these sons and daughters of wealth, a single course of which would feed hundreds of starving ones to whom a full meal of bread washed down by water is a luxury. Look upon these votaries of fashion as they spend their days devising new means of selfish enjoyment — theatres, balls, concerts, yachting, rushing from one part of the globe to another in their mad search for gaiety and pleasure. And then turn a moment and look at those who produce the wealth that pays for these excessive, unnatural enjoyments.

The Other Picture

Look at them herded together in dark, damp cellars, where they never get a breath of fresh air, clothed in rags, carrying their loads of misery from the cradle to the grave, their children running around the streets, naked, starved, without anyone to give them a loving word or tender care, growing up in ignorance and superstition, cursing the day of their birth.

Look at these two startling contrasts, you moralists and philanthropists, and tell me who is to be blamed for it! Those who are driven to prostitution, whether legal or otherwise, or those who drive their victims to such demoralisation?

The cause lies not in prostitution, but in society itself; in the system of inequality of private property and in the State and Church. In the system of legalized theft, murder and violation of the innocent women and helpless children.

The Cure For The Evil

Not until this monster is destroyed will we get rid of the disease which exists in the Senate and all public offices; in the houses of the rich as well as in the miserable barracks of the poor. Mankind must become conscious of their strength and capabilities, they must be free to commence a new life, a better and nobler life.

Prostitution will never be suppressed by the means employed by the Rev. Dr. Parkhurst and other reformers. It will exist as long as the system exists which breeds it.

When all these reformers unite their efforts with those who are striving to abolish the system which begets crime of every description and erect one which is based upon perfect equity — a system which guarantees every member, man, woman or child, the full fruits of their labour and a perfectly equal right to enjoy the gifts of nature and to attain the highest knowledge — woman will be self-supporting and independent. Her health no longer crushed by endless toil and slavery no longer will she be the victim of man, while man will no longer be possessed of unhealthy, unnatural passions and vices.

An Anarchist's Dream

Each will enter the marriage state with physical strength and moral confidence in each other. Each will love and esteem the other, and will help in working not only for their own welfare, but, being happy themselves, they will desire also the universal happiness of humanity. The offspring of such unions will be strong and healthy in mind and body and will honour and respect their parents, not because it is their duty to do so, but because the parents deserve it.

They will be instructed and cared for by the whole community and will be free to follow their own inclinations, and there will be no necessity to teach them sychophancy and the base art of preying upon their fellow-beings. Their aim in life will be, not to obtain power over their brothers, but to win the respect and esteem of every member of the community.

Anarchist Divorce

Should the union of a man and woman prove unsatisfactory and distasteful to them they will in a quiet, friendly manner, separate and not debase the several relations of marriage by continuing an uncongenial union.

If, instead of persecuting the victims, the reformers of the day will unite their efforts to eradicate the cause, prostitution will no longer disgrace humanity.

To suppress one class and protect another is worse than folly. It is criminal. Do not turn away your heads, you moral man and woman.

Do not allow your prejudice to influence you: look at the question from an unbiased standpoint.

Instead of exerting your strength uselessly, join hands and assist to abolish the corrupt, diseased system.

If married life has not robbed you of honour and self-respect, if you have love for those you call your children, you must, for your own sake as well as theirs, seek emancipation and establish liberty. Then, and not until then, will the evils of matrimony cease.

Marriage & Love

The popular notion about marriage and love is that they are synonymous, that they spring from the same motives, and cover the same human needs. Like most popular notions this also rests not on actual facts, but on superstition.

Marriage and love have nothing in common; they are as far apart as the poles; are, in fact, antagonistic to each other. No doubt some marriages have been the result of love. Not, however, because love could assert itself only in marriage; much rather is it because few people can completely outgrow a convention. There are to-day large numbers of men and women to whom marriage is naught but a farce, but who submit to it for the sake of public opinion. At any rate, while it is true that some marriages are based on love, and while it is equally true that in some cases love continues in married life, I maintain that it does so regardless of marriage, and not because of it.

On the other hand, it is utterly false that love results from marriage. On rare occasions one does hear of a miraculous case of a married couple falling in love after marriage, but on close examination it will be found that it is a mere adjustment to the inevitable. Certainly the growing-used to each other is far away from the spontaneity, the intensity, and beauty of love, without which the intimacy of marriage must prove degrading to both the woman and the man.

Marriage is primarily an economic arrangement, an insurance pact. It differs from the ordinary life insurance agreement only in that it is more binding, more exacting. Its returns are insignificantly small compared with the investments. In taking out an insurance policy one pays for it in dollars and cents, always at liberty to discontinue payments. If, how ever, woman's premium is a husband, she pays for it with her name, her privacy, her self-respect, her very life, "until death doth part." Moreover, the marriage insurance condemns her to life-long dependency, to parasitism, to complete uselessness, individual as well as social. Man, too, pays his toll, but as his sphere is wider, marriage does not limit him as much as woman. He feels his chains more in an economic sense.

Thus Dante's motto over Inferno applies with equal force to marriage: "Ye who enter here leave all hope behind."

That marriage is a failure none but the very stupid will deny. One has but to glance over the statistics of divorce to realize how bitter a failure marriage really is. Nor will the stereotyped Philistine argument that the laxity of divorce laws and the growing looseness of woman account for the fact that: first, every twelfth marriage ends in divorce; second, that since 1870 divorces have increased from 28 to 73 for every hundred thousand population;

third, that adultery, since 1867, as ground for divorce, has increased 270.8 per cent.; fourth, that desertion increased 369.8 per cent.

Added to these startling figures is a vast amount of material, dramatic and literary, further elucidating this subject. Robert Herrick, in Together; Pinero, in Mid-Channel; Eugene Walter, in Paid in Full, and scores of other writers are discussing the barrenness, the monotony, the sordidness, the inadequacy of marriage as a factor for harmony and understanding.

The thoughtful social student will not content himself with the popular superficial excuse for this phenomenon. He will have to dig down deeper into the very life of the sexes to know why marriage proves so disastrous.

Edward Carpenter says that behind every marriage stands the life-long environment of the two sexes; an environment so different from each other that man and woman must remain strangers. Separated by an insurmountable wall of superstition, custom, and habit, marriage has not the potentiality of developing knowledge of, and respect for, each other, without which every union is doomed to failure.

Henrik Ibsen, the hater of all social shams, was probably the first to realize this great truth. Nora leaves her husband, not—as the stupid critic would have it—because she is tired of her responsibilities or feels the need of woman's rights, but because she has come to know that for eight years she had lived with a stranger and borne him children. Can there be any thing more humiliating, more degrading than a life long proximity between two strangers? No need for the woman to know anything of the man, save his income. As to the knowledge of the woman—what is there to know except that she has a pleasing appearance? We have not yet outgrown the theologic myth that woman has no soul, that she is a mere appendix to man, made out of his rib just for the convenience of the gentleman who was so strong that he was afraid of his own shadow.

Perchance the poor quality of the material whence woman comes is responsible for her inferiority. At any rate, woman has no soul—what is there to know about her? Besides, the less soul a woman has the greater her asset as a wife, the more readily will she absorb herself in her husband. It is this slavish acquiescence to man's superiority that has kept the marriage institution seemingly intact for so long a period. Now that woman is coming into her own, now that she is actually growing aware of herself as a being outside of the master's grace, the sacred institution of marriage is gradually being undermined, and no amount of sentimental lamentation can stay it.

From infancy, almost, the average girl is told that marriage is her ultimate goal; therefore her training and education must be directed towards that end. Like the mute beast fattened for slaughter, she is prepared for that. Yet, strange to say, she is allowed to know much less about her function as wife and mother than the ordinary artisan of his trade. It is indecent and filthy for a respectable girl to know anything of the marital relation. Oh, for the inconsistency of respectability, that needs the marriage vow to turn something which is filthy into the purest and most sacred arrangement that none dare question or criticize. Yet that is exactly the attitude of the average upholder of marriage. The prospective wife and mother is kept in complete ignorance of her only asset in the competitive field---sex. Thus she enters into life-long relations with a man only to find herself shocked, repelled, outraged beyond measure by the most natural and healthy instinct, sex. It is safe to say that a large percentage of the unhappiness, misery, distress, and physical suffering of matrimony is due to the criminal ignorance in sex matters that is being extolled as a great virtue. Nor is it at all an exaggeration when I say that more than one home has been broken up because of this deplorable fact.

If, however, woman is free and big enough to learn the mystery of sex without the sanction of State or Church, she will stand condemned as utterly unfit to become the wife of a "good" man, his goodness consisting of an empty head and plenty of money. Can there be anything more outrageous than the idea that a healthy, grown woman, full of life and passion, must deny nature's demand, must subdue her most intense craving, undermine her health and break her spirit, must stunt her vision, abstain from the depth and glory of sex experience until a "good" man comes along to take her unto himself as a wife? That is precisely what marriage means. How can such an arrangement end except in failure? This is one, though not the least important, factor of marriage, which differentiates it from love.

Ours is a practical age. The time when Romeo and Juliet risked the wrath of their fathers for love when Gretchen exposed herself to the gossip of her neighbors for love, is no more. If, on rare occasions young people allow themselves the luxury of romance they are taken in care by the elders, drilled and pounded until they become "sensible."

The moral lesson instilled in the girl is not whether the man has aroused her love, but rather is it, "How much?" The important and only God of practical American life: Can the man make a living? Can he support a wife? That is the only thing that justifies marriage. Gradually this saturates every thought of the girl; her dreams are not of moonlight and kisses, of laughter and tears; she dreams of shopping tours and bargain counters. This soul-poverty and sordidness are the elements inherent in the marriage institution. The State and the Church approve of no other ideal, simply because it is the one that necessitates the State and Church control of men and women.

Doubtless there are people who continue to consider love above dollars and cents. Particularly is this true of that class whom economic necessity has forced to become self-supporting. The tremendous change in woman's position, wrought by that mighty factor, is indeed phenomenal when we reflect that it is but a short time since she has entered the industrial arena. Six million women wage-earners; six million women, who have the equal right with men to be exploited, to be robbed, to go on strike; aye, to starve even. Anything more, my lord? Yes, six million age-workers in every walk of life, from the highest brain work to the most difficult menial labor in the mines and on the railroad tracks; yes, even detectives and policemen. Surely the emancipation is complete.

Yet with all that, but a very small number of the vast army of women wage-workers look upon work as a permanent issue, in the same light as does man. No matter how decrepit the latter, he has been taught to be independent, self-supporting. Oh, I know that no one is really independent in our economic tread mill; still, the poorest specimen of a man hates to be a parasite; to be known as such, at any rate.

The woman considers her position as worker transitory, to be thrown aside for the first bidder. That is why it is infinitely harder to organize women than men. "Why should I join a union? I am going to get married, to have a home." Has she not been taught from infancy to look upon that as her ultimate calling? She learns soon enough that the home, though not so large a prison as the factory, has more solid doors and bars. It has a keeper so faithful that naught can escape him. The most tragic part, however, is that the home no longer frees her from wage slavery; it only increases her task.

According to the latest statistics submitted before a Committee "on labor and wages, and congestion of Population," ten per cent. of the wage workers in New York City alone are married, yet they must continue to work at the most poorly paid labor in the world. Add to this horrible aspect the drudgery of house work, and what remains of the protection and glory of the home? As a matter of fact, even the middle class girl in marriage can not speak of her home, since it is the man who creates her sphere. It is not important whether the husband is a brute or a darling. What I wish to prove is that marriage guarantees woman a home only by the grace of her husband. There she moves about in his home, year after year until her aspect of life and human affairs becomes as flat, narrow, and drab as her surroundings. Small wonder if she becomes a nag, petty, quarrelsome, gossipy, unbearable, thus driving the man from the house. She could not go, if she wanted to; there is no place to go. Besides, a short period of married life, of complete surrender of all faculties, absolutely incapacitates the average woman for the outside world. She becomes reckless in appearance, clumsy in her movements, dependent in her decisions, cowardly in her judgment, a weight and a bore, which most men grow to hate and despise. Wonderfully inspiring atmosphere for the bearing of life, is it not?

But the child, how is it to be protected, if not for marriage? After all, is not that the most important consideration? The sham, the hypocrisy of it! Marriage protecting the child, yet thousands of children destitute and homeless. Marriage protecting the child, yet orphan asylums and reformatories over crowded, the Society for the Prevention of Cruelty to Children keeping busy in rescuing the little victims from "loving" parents, to place them under more loving care, the Gerry Society. Oh, the mockery of it!

Marriage may have the power to "bring the horse to water," but has it ever made him drink? The law will place the father under arrest, and put him in convict's clothes; but has that ever stilled the hunger of the child? If the parent has no work, or if he hides his identity, what does marriage do then? It invokes the law to bring the man to "justice," to put him safely behind closed doors; his labor, however, goes not to the child, but to the State. The child receives but a blighted memory of its father's stripes.

As to the protection of the woman,--therein lies the curse of marriage. Not that it really protects her, but the very idea is so revolting, such an outrage and insult on life, so degrading to human dignity, as to forever condemn this parasitic institution.

It is like that other paternal arrangement ---capitalism. It robs man of his birthright, stunts his growth, poisons his body, keeps him in ignorance, in poverty and dependence, and then institutes charities that thrive on the last vestige of man's self-respect.

The institution of marriage makes a parasite of woman, an absolute dependent. It incapacitates her for life's struggle, annihilates her social consciousness, paralyzes her imagination, and then imposes its gracious protection, which is in reality a snare, a travesty on human character.

If motherhood is the highest fulfillment of woman's nature, what other protection does it need save love and freedom? Marriage but defiles, outrages, and corrupts her fulfillment. Does it not say to woman, Only when you follow me shall you bring forth life? Does it not condemn her to the block, does it not degrade and shame her if she refuses to buy her right to motherhood by selling herself? Does not marriage only sanction motherhood, even though conceived in hatred, in compulsion? Yet, if motherhood be of free choice, of love, of ecstasy, of defiant passion, does it not place a crown of thorns upon an innocent head and carve in letters of blood the hideous epithet, Bastard? Were marriage to contain all the virtues claimed for it, its crimes against motherhood would exclude it forever from the realm of love.

Love, the strongest and deepest element in all life, the harbinger of hope, of joy, of ecstasy; love, the defier of all laws, of all conventions; love, the freest, the most powerful moulder of human destiny; how can such an all-compelling force be synonymous with that poor little State and Church-begotten weed, marriage?

Free love? As if love is anything but

free! Man has bought brains, but all the millions in the world have failed to buy love. Man has subdued bodies, but all the power on earth has been unable to subdue love. Man has conquered whole nations, but all his armies could not conquer love. Man has chained and fettered the spirit, but he has been utterly helpless before love. High on a throne, with all the splendor and pomp his gold can command, man is yet poor and desolate, if love passes him by. And if it stays, the poorest hovel is radiant with warmth, with life and color. Thus love has the magic power to make of a beggar a king. Yes, love is free; it can dwell in no other atmosphere. In freedom it gives itself unreservedly, abundantly, completely. All the laws on the statutes, all the courts in the universe, cannot tear it from the soil, once love has taken root. If, however, the soil is sterile, how can marriage make it bear fruit? It is like the last desperate struggle of fleeting life against death.

Love needs no protection; it is its own

protection. So long as love begets life no child is deserted, or hungry, or famished for the want of affection. I know this to be true. I know women who became mothers in freedom by the men they loved. Few children in wedlock enjoy the care, the protection, the devotion free motherhood is capable of bestowing.

The defenders of authority dread the advent of a free motherhood, lest it will rob them of their prey. Who would fight wars? Who would create wealth? Who would make the policeman, the jailer, if woman were to refuse the indiscriminate breeding of children? The race, the race! shouts the king, the president, the capitalist, the priest. The race must be preserved, though woman be degraded to a mere machine, — and the marriage institution is our only safety valve against the pernicious sex-awakening of woman. But in vain these frantic efforts to maintain a state of bondage. In vain, too, the edicts of the Church, the mad attacks of rulers, in vain even the arm of the law. Woman no longer wants to be a party to the production of a race of sickly, feeble, decrepit, wretched human beings, who have neither the strength nor moral courage to throw off the yoke of poverty and slavery. Instead she desires fewer and better children, begotten and reared in love and through free choice; not by compulsion, as marriage imposes. Our pseudo-moralists have yet to learn the deep sense of responsibility toward the child, that love in freedom has awakened in the breast of woman. Rather would she forego forever the glory of motherhood than bring forth life in an atmosphere that breathes only destruction and death. And if she does become a mother, it is to give to the child the deepest and best her being can yield. To grow with the child is her motto; she knows that in that manner alone call she help build true manhood and womanhood.

Ibsen must have had a vision of a free mother, when, with a master stroke, he portrayed Mrs. Alving. She was the ideal mother because she had outgrown marriage and all its horrors, because she had broken her chains, and set her spirit free to soar until it returned a personality, regenerated and strong. Alas, it was too late to rescue her life's joy, her Oswald; but not too late to realize that love in freedom is the only condition of a beautiful life. Those who, like Mrs. Alving, have paid with blood and tears for their spiritual awakening, repudiate marriage as an imposition, a shallow, empty mockery. They know, whether love last but one brief span of time or for eternity, it is the only creative, inspiring, elevating basis for a new race, a new world.

In our present pygmy state love is indeed a stranger to most people. Misunderstood and shunned, it rarely takes root; or if it does, it soon withers and dies. Its delicate fiber can not endure the stress and strain of the daily grind. Its soul is too complex to adjust itself to the slimy woof of our social fabric. It weeps and moans and suffers with those who have need of it, yet lack the capacity to rise to love's summit.

Some day, some day men and women will rise, they will reach the mountain peak, they will meet big and strong and free, ready to receive, to partake, and to bask in the golden rays of love. What fancy, what imagination, what poetic genius can foresee even approximately the potentialities of such a force in the life of men and women. If the world is ever to give birth to true companionship and oneness, not marriage, but love will be the parent.

Jealousy: Causes & a Possible Cure

No one at all capable of an intense conscious inner life need ever hope to escape mental anguish and suffering. Sorrow and often despair over the so-called eternal fitness of things are the most persistent companions of our life. But they do not come upon us from the outside, through the evil deeds of particularly evil people. They are conditioned in our very being; indeed, they are interwoven through a thousand tender and coarse threads with our existence.

It is absolutely necessary that we realize this fact, because people who never get away from the notion that their misfortune is due to the wickedness of their fellows never can outgrow the petty hatred and malice which constantly blames, condemns, and hounds others for something that is inevitable as part of themselves. Such people will not rise to the lofty heights of the true humanitarian to whom good and evil, moral and immoral, are but limited terms for the inner play of human emotions upon the human sea of life.

The "beyond good and evil" philosopher, Nietzsche, is at present denounced as the perpetrator of national hatred and machine gun destruction; but only bad readers and bad pupils interpret him so. "Beyond good and evil" means beyond prosecution, beyond judging, beyond killing, etc. Beyond Good and Evil opens before our eyes a vista the background of which is individual assertion combined with the understanding of all others who are unlike ourselves, who are different.

By that I do not mean the clumsy attempt of democracy to regular the complexities of human character by means of external equality. The vision of "beyond good and evil" points to the right to oneself, to one's personality. Such possibilities do not exclude pain over the chaos of life, but they do exclude the puritanic righteousness that sits in judgment on all others except oneself.

It is self-evident that the thoroughgoing radical — there are many half-baked ones, you know — must apply this deep, humane recognition to the sex and love relation. Sex emotions and love are among the most intimate, the most intense and sensitive, expressions of our being. They are so deeply related to individual physical and psychic traits as to stamp each love affair an independent affair, unlike any other love affair. In other words, each love is the result of the impressions and characteristics the two people involved give to it. Every love relation should by its very nature remain an absolutely private affair. Neither the State, the Church, morality, or people should meddle with it.

Unfortunately this is not the case. The most intimate relation is subject to proscriptions, regulations, and coercions, yet these external factors are absolutely alien to love, and as such lead to everlasting contradictions and conflict between love and law.

The result of it is that our love life is merged into corruption and degradation. "Pure love," so much hailed by the poets, is in the present matrimonial, divorce, and alienation wrangles, a rare specimen indeed. With money, social standing, and position as the criteria for love, prostitution is quite inevitable, even if it be covered with the mantle of legitimacy and morality.

The most prevalent evil of our mutilated love-life is jealousy, often described as the "green-eyed monster" who lies, cheats, betrays, and kills. The popular notion is that jealousy is inborn and therefore can never be eradicated from the human heart. This idea is a convenient excuse for those who lack ability and willingness to delve into cause and effect.

Anguish over a lost love, over the broken thread of love's continuity, is indeed inherent in our very beings. Emotional sorrow has inspired many sublime lyrics, much profound insight and poetic exultation of a Byron, Shelley, Heine, and their kind. But will anyone compare this grief with what commonly passes as jealousy? They are as unlike as wisdom and stupidity. As refinement and coarseness. As dignity and brutal coercion. Jealousy is the very reverse of understanding, of sympathy, and of generous feeling. Never has jealousy added to character, never does it make the individual big and fine. What it really does is to make him blind with fury, petty with suspicion, and harsh with envy.

Jealousy, the contortions of which we see in the matrimonial tragedies and comedies, is invariably a one-sided, bigoted accuser, convinced of his own righteousness and the meanness, cruelty, and guilt of his victim. Jealousy does not even attempt to understand. Its one desire is to punish, and to punish as severely as possible. This notion is embodied in the code of honor, as represented in dueling or the unwritten law. A code which will have it that the seduction of a woman must be atoned with the death of the seducer. Even where seduction has not taken place, where both have voluntarily yielded to the innermost urge, honor is restored only when blood has been shed, either that of the man or the woman.

Jealousy is obsessed by the sense of possession and vengeance. It is quite in accord with all other punitive laws upon the statutes which still adhere to the barbarous notion that an offence, often merely the result of social wrongs, must be adequately punished or revenged.

A very strong argument against jealousy is to be found in the data of historians like Morgan, Reclus, and others, as to the sex relations among primitive people. Anyone at all conversant with their works knows that monogamy is a much later sex from which came into being as a result of the domestication and ownership of women, and which created sex monopoly and the inevitable feeling of jealousy.

In the past, when men and women intermingled freely without interference of law and morality, there could be no jealousy, because the latter rests upon the assumption that a certain man has an exclusive sex monopoly over a certain woman and vice-versa. The moment anyone dates to trespass this sacred precept, jealousy is up in arms. Under such circumstances it is ridiculous to say that jealousy is perfectly natural. As a matter of fact, it is the artificial result of an artificial cause, nothing else.

Unfortunately, it is not only conservative marriages which are saturated with the notion of sex monopoly; the so-called free unions are also victims of it. The argument may be raised that this is one more proof that jealousy is an inborn trait. But it must be borne in mind that sex monopoly has been handed down from generation to generation as a sacred right and the basis of purity of the family and the home. And just as the Church and the State accepted sex monopoly as the only security to the marriage tie, so have both justified jealousy as the legitimate weapon of defense for the protection of the property right.

Now, while it is true that a great many people have outgrown the legality of sex monopoly, they have not outgrown its traditions and habits. Therefore they become as blinded by the "green-eyed monster" as their conservative neighbors the moment their possessions are at stake.

A man or woman free and big enough not to interfere or fuss over the outside attractions of the loved one is sure to be despised by his conservative, and ridiculed by his radical, friends. He will either be decried as a degenerate or a coward; often enough some petty material motives will be imputed to him. In any even, such men and women will be the target of coarse gossip or filthy jokes for no other reason than that they concede to wife, husband or lovers the right to their own bodies and their emotional expression, without making jealous scenes or wild threats to kill the intruder.

There are other factors in jealousy: the conceit of the male and the envy of the female. The male in matters sexual is an imposter, a braggart, who forever boasts of his exploits and success with women. He insists on playing the part of a conqueror, since he has been told that women want to be conquered, that they love to be seduced. Feeling himself the only cock in the barnyard, or the bull who must clash horns in order to win the cow, he feels mortally wounded in his conceit and arrogance the moment a rival appears on the scene — the scene, even among so-called refined men, continues to be woman's sex love, which must belong to only one master.

In other words, the endangered sex monopoly together with man's outraged vanity in ninety-nine cases out of a hundred are the antecedents of jealousy.

In the case of a woman, economic fear for herself and children and her petty envy of every other woman who gains grace in the eyes of her supporter invariably create jealousy. In justice to women be it said that for centuries past, physical attraction was her only stock in trade, therefore she must needs become envious of the charm and value of other women as threatening her hold upon her precious property.

The grotesque aspect of the whole matter is that men and women often grow violently jealous of those they really do not care much about. It is therefore not their outraged love, but their outraged conceit and envy which cry out against this "terrible wrong." Likely as not the woman never loved the man whom she now suspects and spies upon. Likely as not she never made an effort to keep his love. But the moment a competitor arrives, she begins to value her sex property for the defense of which no means are too despicable or cruel.

Obviously, then, jealousy is not the result of love. In fact, if it were possible to investigate most cases of jealousy, it would likely be found that the less people are imbued with a great love the more violent and contemptible is their jealousy. Two people bound by inner harmony and oneness are not afraid to impair their mutual confidence and security if one or the other has outside attractions, nor will their relations end in vile enmity, as is too often the case with many people. They many not be able, nor ought they to be expected, to receive the choice of the loved one into the intimacy of their lives, but that does not give either one the right to deny the necessity of the attraction.

As I shall discuss variety and monogamy two weeks from tonight, I will not dwell upon either here, except to say that to look upon people who can love more than one person as perverse or abnormal is to be very ignorant indeed. I have already discussed a number of causes for jealousy to which I must add the institution of marriage which the State and Church proclaim as "the bond until death doth part." This is accepted as the ethical mode of right living and right doing.

With love, in all its variability and

changeability, fettered and cramped, it is small wonder if jealousy arises out of it. What else but pettiness, meanness, suspicion, and rancor can come when a man and wife are officially held together with the formula "from now on you are one in body and spirit." Just take any couple tied together in such a manner, dependent upon each other for every thought and feeling, without an outside interest or desire, and ask yourself whether such a relation must not become hateful and unbearable in time.

In some form or other the fetters are broken, and as the circumstances which bring this about are usually low and degrading, it is hardly surprising that they bring into play the shabbiest and meanest human traits and motives.

In other words, legal, religious, and moral interference are the parents of our present unnatural love and sex life, and out of it jealousy has grown. It is the lash which whips and tortures poor mortals because of their stupidity, ignorance, and prejudice.

But no one need attempt to justify himself on the ground of being a victim of these conditions. It is only too true that we all smart under the burdens of iniquitous social arrangements, under coercion and moral blindness. But are we not conscious individuals, whose aim it is to bring truth and justice into human affairs? The theory that man is a product of conditions has led only to indifference and to a sluggish acquiescence in these conditions. Yet everyone knows that adaptation to an unhealthy and unjust mode of life only strengthens both, while man, the so-called crown of all creation, equipped with a capacity to think and see and above all to employ his powers of initiative, grows ever weaker, more passive, more fatalistic.

There is nothing more terrible and fatal than to dig into the vitals of one's loved ones and oneself. It can only help to tear whatever slender threads of affection still inhere in the relation and finally bring us to the last ditch, which jealousy attempts to prevent, namely, the annihilation of love, friendship and respect.

Jealousy is indeed a poor medium to secure love, but it is a secure medium to destroy one's self-respect. For jealous people, like dope-fiends, stoop to the lowest level and in the end inspire only disgust and loathing.

Anguish over the loss of love or a nonreciprocated love among people who are capable of high and fine thoughts will never make a person coarse. Those who are sensitive and fine have only to ask themselves whether they can tolerate any obligatory relation, and an emphatic no would be the reply. But most people continue to live near each other although they have long ceased to live with each other — a life fertile enough for the operation of jealousy, whose methods go all the way from opening private correspondence to murder. Compared with such horrors, open adultery seems an act of courage and liberation.

A strong shield against the vulgarity

of jealousy is that man and wife are not of one body and one spirit. They are two human beings, of different temperament, feelings, and emotions. Each is a small cosmos in himself, engrossed in his own thoughts and ideas. It is glorious and poetic if these two worlds meet in freedom and equality. Even if this lasts but a short time it is already worthwhile. But, the moment the two worlds are forced together all the beauty and fragrance ceases and nothing but dead leaves remain. Whoever grasps this truism will consider jealousy beneath him and will not permit it to hang as a sword of Damocles over him.

All lovers do well to leave the doors of their love wide open. When love can go and come without fear of meeting a watch-dog, jealousy will rarely take root because it will soon learn that where there are no locks and keys there is no place for suspicion and distrust, two elements upon which jealousy thrives and prospers.

An Unexpected Dash Through Spain

Sitting tucked away in quiet St. Tropez, at work on my autobiography, I was as far from the thought of a trip to Spain as if I had been living in Tokio, Shanghai or Kamchatka. I did plan a rest away from my book during the Christmas holidays. One needs a break, even in the most ideal love life, and the process of reliving and writing one's past is anything but ideal. Au contraire, as we say in France! It is very painful, with much of the bitter and nothing of the sweet that love represents. Writing strenuously for five months entitled me to a rest; even my enemies couldn't grudge me that. And what other city in Europe is so enticing as Paris, even if the winter weather is rotten? It was Paris, then, for a month.

No one ever quite completely escapes the power of suggestion, at least if the suggestors are good friends and interested in one's development and morals, and when the suggestion holds out a trip through Spain. It is not often that a lady of questionable age is offered the chaperonship of two gentlemen friends — one very young, the other very handsome. As is the habit of my sex, I changed my mind — and Paris for Spain.

It was a mad rush. In nineteen days, of which considerable time was spent in trains and busses, and thirty-six hours in Tangier, we visited ten cities — 'dashed through' would express it more accurately. Alas, there was hardly time to get one's breath, let alone to really get close to the heart of a stern and aloof country like Spain. One could but skim the surface.

Besides my interest in the new land, its famed art treasures, I longed to see some of the revolutionary spirit which I had heard and read about so much. Whatever there was of it has no doubt been driven underground by the dictatorship. Certainly there was no sign of it anywhere. The most astounding thing about the Spanish dictator is that he has no organized backing like the Italian Caesar, at least we were assured of that by everyone who felt free to talk to us about the political situation. I myself was able to see only the comrades, and very few among them. But one of the friends I was with interviewed a number of people representing different factions — Republicans, Nationalists, Socialists, Communists, — workers and intellectuals. All assured him in one voice that no one wanted the dictatorship. But these people could give no adequate explanation as to how the much-hated and undersired dictator, could keep his one-man job so long.

I confess even our own comrades failed to convince me how it was possible for one man to destroy not only the revolutionary labor movement but every educational, literary and cultural attempt of a liberal nature as well. Not a trace is left of Ferrer's great work! Of course there is the church and the king — there is the army, although the recent uprising in some of the garrisons would prove that all is not pro-Rivera even there — and there is a terrifically large police force. The question is, when have these sinister forces not been in Spain? They have always done their deadly work. Their existence is not of recent date, therefore they could not be taken as the only explanation for the dictatorship.

It seems to me that there is a deeper cause for the crushing political situation in Spain — a cause not only in Spain, but one of universal magnitude. It is the hydra-headed monster Reaction, the child of the war, born from its womb and nourished by its blood. This reaction exists in all ranks, the masses and the workers not excluded. There is no use closing our eyes to a world phenomena, and it is foolish to put all the blame on one class, the ruling party. The slaves no less than their masters are now prostrate before the monster Dictatorship. If proofs were wanted, Italy and Spain are living examples.

In these two countries revolutionary ideas have not been grafted on the people by a handful of the intelligentsia, as in Russia for instance. Here they have had their roots in the life and activities of the mass itself. One would have expected them to resist the onslaught of the dictatorship, yet they did nothing of the kind. True, the conscious minority has retained its revolutionary fibre, and is now filling the prisons. But the fact that Mussolini and Rivera could swing themselves so easily into the saddle and continue to hold the reins for so long shows that revolutionary ideals must have been frail plants that they could have been quickly uprooted.

Yes, the Church of Spain is all-powerful. One does not have to be there long to see that. Its force was brought home by the remark of a cultured old Jew, a man who has lived in Spain for fifty years. He said it was impossible to talk confidentially to any Spaniard, because the latter would report what was said to his wife, who would in turn confess it to her priest. Or, as a Spanish churchman expressed himself: "We do not care if we have the men, so long as we can influence the women." What he failed to say was that the church in Spain can count on the women because the men want them to continue in an abject and ignorant state.

It seems unbelievable in our time of woman's progress to find such an antiquated attitude towards women as that display from Spanish men. From our own comrades and from people in quite different camps I learned that Spain is today what other countries were fifty years ago. The place of woman is still only in the home — her function only the breeding of children. I had occasion to verify both. Going into a cafe with the young wife of an American correspondent was like running the gauntlet. There was hardly a man in the packed place, who did not rise and stare at the phenomenon of two women (one by no means in her teens) daring to enter a cafe without a male escort. On the other hand it was nothing unusual to see women with troops of children, no more than a year apart promenading in the streets. With women still in such a condition, they would naturally represent the bulwark of the church. Ignorance and submission have ever been the strongest support of the priesthood.

The most stirring experience of my trip, outside of the art treasures I saw, was my meeting with our beautiful comrades, F. U. and his wife and daughter, and the Louise Michel of Spain, Therese Claramoun. These people are among the last surviving victims of the horrors of Montjuich. Seeing and talking with these dear comrades brought to life again the crime of Canovas del Castilla, prime minister of Spain, who was responsible for the reinstatement of the Inquisition in 1897. An the thought of Angiolillo came back to me, in his simple and heroic greatness. It was he who gave his life in return for taking that of Canovas.

Never in my wildest fancy did I ever

think I would be so close to any of the victims whose cause I had pleaded so earnestly thirty-two years ago. And now I was in their house, at their table, enjoying their sweet hospitality. It seemed like a dream.

I was moved most deeply by Therese, now sixty-five years of age. More than half of her life she had been active in our movement, she had spent many years in prison and in exile. But her spirit was like a white flame; nothing but death will extinguish its fires. With remarkable clarity she related some of the incidents of the terrible period in Montjuich — the tortures innocent men were submitted to — the anguish of those, who though not tortured themselves, could still do nothing for their comrades. She spoke of one of the victims who had to be supported in court, his poor body battered and burned by the henchmen of Canovas. Over the judges bench hung the image of Jesus. The deep-set, suffering eyes of the prisoner looked searchingly at the Christly figure, then his voice rang out: "O Christian God, what was your agony compared with that your followers have made me suffer!" He was one of the five who were shot, after endless days and nights of torture.

Therese looked shrunken in her armchair, in a cold room, wrapped in blankets, her hands and her legs partly paralyzed. But when she rose to take us to the door she became an imposing figure, still the fighter, yet with infinite charm and graciousness. I came away from this remarkable woman, both inspired and saddened. She is of the old, heroic guard, which is slowly dying out. And where is the young generation to take its place?

The U's have been in the forefront of our movement since 1886 and have lost none of their energy and enthusiasm. They are sustained by their daughter Frederica, being among the very few whose children are imbued with the ideals of their parents. But Frederica is more than that — she is an independent thinker, whose Anarchism is not a mere echo of her parents, but something very powerful which fills her life.

The home of our dear comrades is a real commune. Living with them on equal footing are two young girls, daughters of comrades who are serving long sentences in prison. The father of one of these is Mateo Morales.

Propaganda under the dictatorship is made impossible, yet the U.'s have an extensive publishing house and get out a tremendous amount of educational books, many of them translations. Besides this they also publish a considerable lot of fiction, among which Frederica's own novels have an important place.

With this young and ardent comrade I went out to that terrible fortress, Montjuich Prison. As we climbed the high hill Frederica told me that road was called Calvary, for along this road innumerable prisoners, chains on their wrists and ankles were made to drag their weary bodies in the night to their living grave. Montjuich, reared on a high rock, one side facing the sea, looked singularly like Schlusselburg, the tomb of the brave fighters against Czarism. One thorough thing the Russian Revolution has certainly done — it has completely demolished Schlusselburg. Montjuich still awaits a similar doom. It is to be hoped that if ever the Revolution comes to Spain it will go farther than the Russian one has gone — that it will demolish all prisons, and establish real freedom.

The comrades I saw in Madrid seemed to be in a more harassed position. One had only recently come out of prison and is under constant police surveillance, being obliged to report to the police department every week. The other lives with a wife and six children in three small rooms in great poverty. They are never secure from the police. Fearing that my presence in their quarters might only add to their danger I did not tarry long.

To write of my impressions of the art of Spain, would be entirely too presumptuous after so brief a visit. Each city is rich enough in art treasures to need months of study. The Mosque in Cordova alone — the most typically Spanish city — could be seen an endless number of times — it is so overwhelming in its beauty and grandeur. The Moorish palaces in Seville, the city itself, the cathedral — Granada, with its marvellous specimens of Moorish art — how could one hope to get anything but a jumble of impressions and how could one say anything about them? Then Toledo — one could spend weeks there. The house of the great master El Greco, and his paintings, would alone be worth spending the whole time in seeing — the two synagogues, with much of the old carving in Hebrew letters still intact! When the Moors were conquered and driven out the Jew shared their fate as they had shared their glory, for under the Moors the Jews were a free people, a great force in the land. After the conquest the Church turned one of the synagogues into a house of prostitution, then into a church. The last two have often gone together. Now the synagogues are empty and stand like sentinels of a great past.

In Madrid there is the Prado, the most wonderful museum I have ever seen, containing the richest collection of painting in the world. I was only able to spend four hours there, when one painting of Velasquez alone would require much more than that to appreciate its beauty and the mastery of its technique.

All in all, it was a mad venture to go to Spain for two weeks, yet I would not have missed it for anything. To be able to lift even a corner of the veil of a strange and fascinating world already helps to enlarge one's horizon. The tragedy is that so few people have neither the means nor the will to get out of their own narrow confines. Neither are they reckless enough to go in quest of new worlds and new beauties. But if one is as young as I, and fortunate enough to find two such charming male escorts, it is not difficult to make a dashing and adventurous trip, even these favorable auspices brought me to Paris dazed and weary. Now, however, I am back in quiet St. Tropez, with my face sternly set against pleasure, determined to resume the writing of my autobiography.

St. Tropez, Var. March 1929

Was My Life Worth Living?

I.

How much a personal philosophy is a matter of temperament and how much it results from experience is a moot question. Naturally we arrive at conclusions in the light of our experience, through the application of a process we call reasoning to the facts observed in the events of our lives. The child is susceptible to fantasy. At the same time he sees life more truly in some respects than his elders do as he becomes conscious of his surroundings. He has not yet become absorbed by the customs and prejudices which make up the largest part of what passes for thinking. Each child responds differently to his environment. Some become rebels, refusing to be dazzled by social superstitions.

They are outraged by every injustice perpetrated upon them or upon others. They grow ever more sensitive to the suffering round them and the restriction registering every convention and taboo imposed upon them.

I evidently belong to the first category. Since my earliest recollection of my youth in Russia I have rebelled against orthodoxy in every form. I could never bear to witness harshness whether I was outraged over the official brutality practiced on the peasants in our neighborhood. I wept bitter tears when the young men were conscripted into the army and torn from homes and hearths. I resented the treatment of our servants, who did the hardest work and yet had to put up with wretched sleeping quarters and the leavings of our table. I was indignant when I discovered that love between young people of Jewish and Gentile origin was considered the crime of crimes, and the birth of an illegitimate child the most depraved immorality.

On coming to America I had the same hopes as have most European immigrants and the same disillusionment, though the latter affected me more keenly and more deeply. The immigrant without money and without connections is not permitted to cherish the comforting illusion that America is a benevolent uncle who assumes a tender and impartial guardianship of nephews and nieces. I soon learned that in a republic there are myriad ways by which the strong, the cunning, the rich can seize power and hold it. I saw the many work for small wages which kept them always on the borderline of want for the few who made huge profits. I saw the courts, the halls of legislation, the press, and the schools — in fact every avenue of education and protection — effectively used as an instrument for the safeguarding of a minority, while the masses were denied every right. I found that the politicians knew how to befog every issue, how to control public opinion and manipulate votes to their own advantage and to that of their financial and industrial allies. This was the picture of democracy I soon discovered on my arrival in the United States. Fundamentally there have been few changes since that time.

This situation, which was a matter of daily experience, was brought home to me with a force that tore away shams and made reality stand out vividly and clearly by an event which occurred shortly after my coming to America. It was the so-called Haymarket riot, which resulted in the trial and conviction of eight men, among them five Anarchists. Their crime was an all-embracing love for the fellow-men and their determination to emancipate the oppressed and disinherited masses. In no way had the State of Illinois succeeded in proving their connection with the bomb that had been thrown at an open-air meeting in Haymarket Square in Chicago. It was their Anarchism which resulted in their conviction and execution on the 11th of November, 1887. This judicial crime left an indelible mark on my mind and heart and sent me forth to acquaint myself with the ideal for which these men had died so heroically. I dedicated myself to their cause.

It requires something more than personal experience to gain a philosophy or point of view from any specific event. It is the quality of our response to the event and our capacity to enter into the lives of others that help us to make their lives and experiences our own. In my own case my convictions have derived and developed from events in the lives of others as well as from my own experience. What I have seen meted out to others by authority and repression, economic and political, transcends anything I myself may have endured.

I have often been asked why I maintained such a non-compromising antagonism to government and in what way I have found myself oppressed by it. In my opinion every individual is hampered by it. It exacts taxes from production. It creates tariffs, which prevent free exchange.

It stands ever for the status quo and traditional conduct and belief. It comes into private lives and into most intimate personal relations, enabling the superstitious, puritanical, and distorted ones to impose their ignorant prejudice and moral servitudes upon the sensitive, the imaginative, and the free spirits. Government does this by its divorce laws, its moral censorships, and by a thousand petty persecutions of those who are too honest to wear the moral mask of respectability. In addition, government protects the strong at the expense of the weak, provides courts and laws which the rich may scorn and the poor must obey. It enables the predatory rich to make wars to provide foreign markets for the favored ones, with prosperity for the rulers and wholesale death for the ruled. However, it is not only government in the sense of the state which is destructive of every individual value and quality. It is the whole complex of authority and institutional domination which strangles life. It is the superstition, myth, pretense, evasions, and subservience which support authority and institutional domination. It is the reverence for these institutions instilled in the school, the church and the home in order that man may believe and obey without protest. Such a process of devitalizing and distorting personalities of the individual and of whole communities may have been a part of historical evolution; but it should be strenuously combated by every honest and independent mind in an age which has any pretense to enlightenment.

It has often been suggested to me that the Constitution of the United States is a sufficient safeguard for the freedom of its citizens. It is obvious that even the freedom it pretends to guarantee is very limited. I have not been impressed with the adequacy of the safeguard. The nations of the world, with centuries of international law behind them, have never hesitated to engage in mass destruction when solemnly pledged to keep the peace; and the legal documents in America have not prevented the United States from doing the same. Those in authority have and always will abuse their power. And the instances when they do not do so are as rare as roses growing on icebergs. Far from the Constitution playing any liberating part in the lives of the American people, it has robbed them of the capacity to rely on their own resources or do their own thinking. Americans are so easily hoodwinked by the sanctity of law and authority. In fact, the pattern of life has become standardized, routinized, and mechanized like canned food and Sunday sermons. The hundred-percenter easily swallows syndicated information and factory-made ideas and beliefs. He thrives on the wisdom given him over the radio and cheap magazines by corporations whose philanthropic aim is selling America out. He accepts the standards of conduct and art in the same breath with the advertising of chewing gum, toothpaste, and shoe polish. Even songs are turned out like buttons or automobile tires — all cast from the same mold.

II.

Yet I do not despair of American life. On the contrary, I feel that the freshness of the American approach and the untapped stores of intellectual and emotional energy resident in the country offer much promise for the future. The War has left in its wake a confused generation. The madness and brutality they had seen, the needless cruelty and waste which had almost wrecked the world made them doubt the values their elders had given them. Some, knowing nothing of the world's past, attempted to create new forms of life and art from the air. Others experimented with decadence and despair. Many of them, even in revolt, were pathetic. They were thrust back into submission and futility because they were lacking in an ideal and were further hampered by a sense of sin and the burden of dead ideas in which they could no longer believe.

Of late there has been a new spirit manifested in the youth which is growing up with the depression. This spirit is more purposeful though still confused. It wants to create a new world, but is not clear as to how it wants to go about it. For that reason the young generation asks for saviors. It tends to believe in dictators and to hail each new aspirant for that honor as a messiah. It wants cut and dried systems of salvation with a wise minority to direct society on some one-way road to utopia. It has not yet realized that it must save itself. The young generation has not yet learned that the problems confronting them can be solved only by themselves and will have to be settled on the basis of social and economic freedom in co-operation with the struggling masses for the right to the table and joy of life.

As I have already stated, my objection to authority in whatever form has been derived from a much larger social view, rather than from anything I myself may have suffered from it. Government has, of course, interfered with my full expression, as it has with others. Certainly the powers have not spared me. Raids on my lectures during my thirty-five years' activity in the United States were a common occurrence, followed by innumerable arrests and three convictions to terms of imprisonment. This was followed by the annulment of my citizenship and my deportation. The hand of authority was forever interfering with my life. If I have none the less expressed myself, it was in spite of every curtailment and difficulty put in my path and not because of them. In that I was by no means alone. The whole world has given heroic figures to humanity, who in the face of persecution and obloquy have lived and fought for their right and the right of mankind to free and unstinted expression. America has the distinction of having contributed a large quota of native-born children who have most assuredly not lagged behind. Walt Whitman, Henry David Thoreau, Voltairine de Cleyre, one of America's great Anarchists, Moses Harman, the pioneer of woman's emancipation from sexual bondage, Horace Traubel, sweet singer of liberty, and quite an array of other brave souls have expressed themselves in keeping with their vision of a new social order based on freedom from every form of coercion. True, the price they had to pay was high. They were deprived of most of the comforts society offers to ability and talent, but denies when they will not be subservient. But whatever the price, their lives were enriched beyond the common lot. I, too, feel enriched beyond measure. But that is due to the discovery of Anarchism, which more than anything else has strengthened my conviction that authority stultifies human development, while full freedom assures it.

I consider Anarchism the most beautiful and practical philosophy that has yet been thought of in its application to individual expression and the relation it establishes between the individual and society. Moreover, I am certain that Anarchism is too vital and too close to human nature ever to die. It is my conviction that dictatorship, whether to the right or to the left, can never work — that it never has worked, and that time will prove this again, as it has been proved before. When the failure of modern dictatorship and authoritarian philosophies becomes more apparent and the realization of failure more general, Anarchism will be vindicated. Considered from this point, a recrudescence of Anarchist ideas in the near future is very probable. When this occurs and takes effect, I believe that humanity will at last leave the maze in which it is now lost and will start on the path to sane living and regeneration through freedom.

There are many who deny the possibility of such regeneration on the ground that human nature cannot change. Those who insist that human nature remains the same at all times have learned nothing and forgotten nothing. They certainly have not the faintest idea of the tremendous strides that have been made in sociology and psychology, proving beyond a shadow of a doubt that human nature is plastic and can be changed. Human nature is by no means a fixed quantity. Rather, it is fluid and responsive to new conditions. If, for instance, the so-called instinct of self-preservation were as fundamental as it is supposed to be, wars would have been eliminated long ago, as would all dangerous and hazardous occupations.

Right here I want to point out that there would not be such great changes required as is commonly supposed to insure the success of a new social order, as conceived by Anarchists. I feel that our present equipment would be adequate if the artificial oppressions and inequalities and the organized force and violence supporting them were removed.

Again it is argued that if human nature can be changed, would not the love of liberty be trained out of the human heart? Love of freedom is a universal trait, and no tyranny has thus far succeeded in eradicating it. Some of the modern dictators might try it, and in fact are trying it with every means of cruelty at their command. Even if they should last long enough to carry on such a project — which is hardly conceivable — there are other difficulties. For one thing, the people whom the dictators are attempting to train would have to be cut off from every tradition in their history that might suggest to them the benefits of freedom. They would also have to isolate them from contact with any other people from whom they could get libertarian ideas. The very fact, however, that a person has a consciousness of self, of being different from others, creates a desire to act freely. The craving for liberty and self-expression is a very fundamental and dominant trait.

As is usual when people are trying to get rid of uncomfortable facts, I have often encountered the statement that the average man does not want liberty; that the love for it exists in very few; that the American people, for instance, simply do not care for it. That the American people are not wholly lacking in the desire for freedom was proved by their resistance to the late Prohibition Law, which was so effective that even the politicians finally responded to popular demand and repealed the amendment. If the American masses had been as determined in dealing with more important issues, much more might have been accomplished. It is true, however, that the American people are just beginning to be ready for advanced ideas. This is due to the historical evolution of the country. The rise of capitalism and a very powerful state are, after all, recent in the United States. Many still foolishly believe themselves back in the pioneer tradition when success was easy, opportunities more plentiful than now, and the economic position of the individual was not likely to become static and hopeless.

It is true, none the less, that the average American is still steeped in these traditions, convinced that prosperity will yet return. But because a number of people lack individuality and the capacity for independent thinking I cannot admit that for this reason society must have a special nursery to regenerate them. I would insist that liberty, real liberty, a freer and more flexible society, is the only medium for the development of the best potentialities of the individual.

I will grant that some individuals grow to great stature in revolt against existing conditions. I am only too aware of the fact that my own development was largely in revolt. But I consider it absurd to argue from this fact that social evils should be perpetrated to make revolt against them necessary. Such an argument would be a repetition of the old religious idea of purification. For one thing it is lacking in imagination to suppose that one who shows qualities above the ordinary could have developed only in one way. The person who under this system has developed along the lines of revolt might readily in a different social situation have developed as an artist, scientist, or in any other creative and intellectual capacity.

III.

Now I do not claim that the triumph of my ideas would eliminate all possible problems from the life of man for all time. What I do believe is that the removal of the present artificial obstacles to progress would clear the ground for new conquests and joy of life. Nature and our own complexes are apt to continue to provide us with enough pain and struggle. Why then maintain the needless suffering imposed by our present social structure, on the mythical grounds that our characters are thus strengthened, when broken hearts and crushed lives about us every day give the lie to such a notion?

Most of the worry about the softening of human character under freedom comes from prosperous people. It would be difficult to convince the starving man that plenty to eat would ruin his character. As for individual development in the society to which I look forward, I feel that with freedom and abundance unguessed springs of individual initiative would be released.

Human curiosity and interest in the world could be trusted to develop individuals in every conceivable line of effort.

Of course those steeped in the present find it impossible to realize that gain as an incentive could be replaced by another force that would motivate people to give the best that is in them. To be sure, profit and gain are strong factors in our present system. They have to be. Even the rich feel a sense of insecurity. That is, they want to protect what they have and to strengthen themselves. The gain and profit motives, however, are tied up with more fundamental motives. When a man provides himself with clothes and shelter, if he is the money-maker type, he continues to work to establish his status — to give himself prestige of the sort admired in the eyes of his fellow-men. Under different and more just conditions of life these more fundamental motives could be put to special uses, and the profit motive, which is only their manifestation, will pass away. Even to-day the scientist, inventor, poet, and artist are not primarily moved by the consideration of gain or profit. The urge to create is the first and most impelling force in their lives. If this urge is lacking in the mass of workers it is not at all surprising, for their occupation is deadly routine. Without any relation to their lives or needs, their work is done in the most appalling surroundings, at the behest of those who have the power of life and death over the masses. Why then should they be impelled to give of themselves more than is absolutely necessary to eke out their miserable existence?

In art, science, literature, and in departments of life which we believe to be somewhat removed from our daily living we are hospitable to research, experiment, and innovation. Yet, so great is our traditional reverence for authority that an irrational fear arises in most people when experiment is suggested to them. Surely there is even greater reason for experiment in the social field than in the scientific. It is to be hoped, therefore, that humanity or some portion of it will be given the opportunity in the not too distant future to try its fortune living and developing under an application of freedom corresponding to the early stages of an anarchistic society. The belief in freedom assumes that human beings can co-operate. They do it even now to a surprising extent, or organized society would be impossible. If the devices by which men can harm one another, such as private property, are removed and if the worship of authority can be discarded, co-operation will be spontaneous and inevitable, and the individual will find it his highest calling to contribute to the enrichment of social well-being.

Anarchism alone stresses the importance of the individual, his possibilities and needs in a free society. Instead of telling him that he must fall down and worship before institutions, live and die for abstractions, break his heart and stunt his life for taboos, Anarchism insists that the center of gravity in society is the individual — that he must think for himself, act freely, and live fully. The aim of Anarchism is that every individual in the world shall be able to do so. If he is to develop freely and fully, he must be relieved from the interference and oppression of others. Freedom is, therefore, the cornerstone of the Anarchist philosophy. Of course, this has nothing in common with a much boasted "rugged individualism." Such predatory individualism is really flabby, not rugged. At the least danger to its safety it runs to cover of the state and wails for protection of armies, navies, or whatever devices for strangulation it has at its command. Their "rugged individualism" is simply one of the many pretenses the ruling class makes to unbridled business and political extortion.

Regardless of the present trend toward the strong-armed man, the totalitarian states, or the dictatorship from the left, my ideas have remained unshaken. In fact, they have been strengthened by my personal experience and the world events through the years. I see no reason to change, as I do not believe that the tendency of dictatorship can ever successfully solve our social problems. As in the past, so I do now insist that freedom is the soul of progress and essential to every phase of life. I consider this as near a law of social evolution as anything we can postulate. My faith is in the individual and in the capacity of free individuals for united endeavor.

The fact that the Anarchist movement for which I have striven so long is to a certain extent in abeyance and overshadowed by philosophies of authority and coercion affects me with concern, but not with despair. It seems to me a point of special significance that many countries decline to admit Anarchists. All governments hold the view that while parties of the right and left may advocate social changes, still they cling to the idea of government and authority. Anarchism alone breaks with both and propagates uncompromising rebellion. In the long run, therefore, it is Anarchism which is considered deadlier to the present regime than all other social theories that are now clamoring for power.

Considered from this angle, I think my life and my work have been successful. What is generally regarded as success — acquisition of wealth, the capture of power or social prestige — I consider the most dismal failures. I hold when it is said of a man that he has arrived, it means that he is finished — his development has stopped at that point. I have always striven to remain in a state of flux and continued growth, and not to petrify in a niche of self-satisfaction. If I had my life to live over again, like anyone else, I should wish to alter minor details. But in any of my more important actions and attitudes I would repeat my life as I have lived it. Certainly I should work for Anarchism with the same devotion and confidence in its ultimate triumph.

Other Fine Titles from Trident Press:

Blood-Soaked Buddha/Hard Earth Pascal
by Noah Cicero

it gets cold
by jasper avery

Major Diamonds Nights & Knives
by Katie Foster

Cactus
by Nathaniel Kennon Perkins

Sixty Tattoos I Secretly Gave Myself at Work
by Tanner Ballengee

The Pocket Peter Kropotkin

The Silence is the Noise
by Bart Schaneman

www.ingramcontent.com/pod-product-compliance
Lightning Source LLC
Chambersburg PA
CBHW070929030426
42336CB00014BA/2604